CURIOSISOSITY

GREG BACHAR

Books By Greg Bachar

Three-Sided Coin
(Published Works 1990-2003)
2003

Sensual Eye
(The Jack Waste Papers Volume 1: 2004-1991)
2004

Curiosisosity
2013

Dumb Bell & Sticky Foot
(And Other Indulgences)
2013

Beans
(& Other Sundry Items From The General Store)
2013

The Amusement Park Of The Mind
(Essays On Thought, Feeling, Experience)
2013

The Writing Machine
(Writings On Writing: Occasional Ruminations
On An Intangible Legerdemain)
2013

CURIOSISOSITY

GREG BACHAR

ROWHOUSE PRESS 2013

Acknowledgements

"Be An Otter," "Orange Bloodcrush," "Lickfrog," "The "Wrong Corner," "Conduit," "Finally Myself," "Faces In The Rock Faces" (Conduit), "A Chime For His Ache" (Pontoon Anthology Of WA State Poets), "Inside A Ring," "So Many Wheels And So Many Gallows," "Balthus Invented By Color," "This Ghostly Triangle In The Steropticon," "She Was Russian And Loved Snow" (Hawaii Review), "Amsterdam, 1936" (Indiana Review), "Tired Of Rust And Broken Bones" (Southeast Review), "A Textbook's Shimmy In A Carpenter's Bind," "A Small Bit Of Noise On My Knuckle" (Quick Fiction), "Green Clown On A Black Cross" (Exquisite Corpse Online), "The Careful Forest" (Clare), "Shin Rubble" (Caesura), "The Broth Never Varies," "The Sacred Breadbox" (Dislocate), "Rain" (Bigger Than They Appear: Anthology Of Very Short Poems), "Cluster," "Polyester Spun Red Horse" (Pacific Review), "Yeast" (Amoskeag), "Accidental Sharps & Flats," "Sunday's Best," "Night Crossing" (Arroyo Literary Review), "Gram's Easter Flume Ride," "Up At Nag's Head, Steaming" (Sentence), "Woodchoppers," "Young May Knot," "Orange Grove In A Funhouse Mirror," "A Rusting Hulk," "Eliab's Grave" (Gravel), "Looking For Anti-Honey" (Pageboy), "With Our Molars" (Re-Dactions), "Toehold On A Sheep's Head" (Temenos).

Inquiries:
P.O. Box 23134
Seattle, WA 98102-0434
U.S.A.

ISBN # 0-9719867-3-8

Cover Painting By Stefanie Payne

CURIOSISOSITY

ONE: 47 POEMS

TWO: FRAGMENTS

THREE: THE CAGE WRITINGS

FOUR: THE ORANGE

FIVE: WERTHER'S 47

ONE: 47 POEMS

Unchained by the naturalistic fate of hope…

--Jerry Lewis

FAMOUS FRENCH TREE

We saw a movie about a famous tree in a town not far from the theatre where we learned it had spiral stairs wrapped around its trunk and branches, even the thin little branches near the top, where miniature French filmmakers stood shouting at extras to act more excited about the seeds falling and sprouting little staircase seedlings on the ground, while careful British gardeners sprinkled varnish from rusty tin watering cans grown like potatoes in Czechoslovakia.

After the film and a late night dinner of bubbling farm cider, omelets, crepes, and strong cigarettes, we drove our small rented car to see the tree and its stairs. A sleepy gendarme with a lively moustache shook his head and pointed in the direction from which we had just come.

"But why?" we cried. The gendarme put his fingers to his lips and said: "Hush. Ca Va. Okay. Come with me." He put a hand on our shoulders, led us to the tree, and with the tips of his moustaches, pointed to a spot on the ground illuminated by brass lantern beams where a tiny spiral staircase sprout had just poked the tip of its nose through the surface of the earth.

The gendarme whispered: "It's just taken its first step."

AMSTERDAM, 1936

In spring, when I was a child too young to know that it was spring, the milk cart was pulled by a little dog that barked while the milkman rang his bell. We stuck our heads out the window, hoping to see thick cream skimmed from the top of the wood barrel of still-warm milk. The little dog looked up at us and smiled until the milkman tipped his white cap, whistled, and moved on down the street.

In winter, the milk cart was pulled by an old brown mule with gray cataracts for eyes and long saliva icicles hanging from his chin. We listened from the window without looking because the windows were glazed over with frost. The milk cart never stopped for long when it was cold, but sped on with the milkman cracking his whip, anxious to return the mule to the warmth of its stable. We wondered what had happened to the little dog while we skated on the frozen canals.

In spring and winter, when the difference between seasons was a whistle and a whip, a little dog and an old blind mule, I was a child who didn't know that the milkman had a name other than the milkman, and that he too wondered what had happened to the little dog he'd never bothered to name.

BE AN OTTER

It must be strange to become a Poet, to have learned how to replace all the haggard empties with fill in the blanks. It must be strange to become anything and stay that way for the rest of your life.

There are other ways to survive without having to say: "I Am This" or "I Am That." Why become? And if someone does ask what you are, lie, make something up: if you're a Poet, say you're a Plumber. If you're a Plumber, say you work at the zoo, and that an ostrich was sick today.

ORANGE BLOODCRUSH

Your envelope, your letter, my paper cut. The blood that fell from my window collected itself in a pool of wild street dogs. Untamed, they spilled into the gutter, traipsed through the sewers of the tunnels behind your eyes.

Slowly, they approached the cathedral of bones where you sat laughing. Or were you praying? The difficulty of knowing who you are and who you are to me is the tragedy I wanted to avoid.

I already know too many strangers.

LICKFROG

I saw you in a church. The priest took me to a back room filled with must and fog. In a corner, in a glass aquarium, there were twelve frogs. If you lick these frogs, the priest said, you will be subject to divine visions, you will fall prey to the love you always wanted to be a victim of.

I chose three choice frogs, licked their backs, their legs, and their foreheads, and even though until that moment you didn't know me, you didn't object, flinch, or act like anything was happening that shouldn't be happening when I slid into your pew.

Later, when the headache of my hallucinations went away, you let me stay.

THE WRONG CORNER

I hung out for days at the wrong corner. I should have taken a room above the mannequin store where you worked and dropped a water balloon on your head when you emerged for lunch.

Instead, I closed the phone booth door and sobbed at least two dime's worth of tears into the coin slot. The operator came on the line to tell me I needed another nickel for another three minutes, but there was nothing left inside me except mischief.

That night I broke into your shop, took off my clothes and stood with the mannequins. This is how I was able to spy on you, this is how I knew you ate lunch alone from a brown paper bag, two sandwiches and some grapes. This is how I fell in love with you, how I knew you know the difference between what is real and what is not.

As you were closing your shop's door you turned to me and said: "I'll meet you at the corner in five minutes."

CONDUIT

Noise of your coming arrival, Victory, ticker tape, parade of realized dreams. Sometimes a daisy chain hung on the doorknob of a vacant motel room attracts the laughter of knowing hyenas.

They bring buckets of ice, bibles, and road maps to mark your lover's trail. You push a button. A red light says: She is here, or: She is there, or: She will be where you are, sooner than later, sooner than even now.

There's a knock on the motel door. It's her, she knows you, there's no need for words: you have a whole roll of quarters for the vibrating bed.

FINALLY MYSELF

No one knows that I am nobody. They think that I am somebody, and treat me as such, with equal parts fear and apprehension. To be somebody doing nothing is one thing, but I am nobody doing something, and that confuses them.

They think it odd that a somebody like me would do what I do—none of them listen when I try to tell them I am no one and that although I am doing something, they might as well think of me as doing nothing, since it would be easier to be seen as a nobody that way.

I want to marry a real nobody, someone who means nothing to no one anywhere. That would be something to me, and she would be my everything. My nobody girl, how everybody will love her, thinking her a real somebody like me, but it's nothing, really, just a little of this and a little of that, some crumbs and a piece of ice tied to black string. That, to me, is something.

Show me what you can make of three men looking down into a grave wearing blank expressions and G-Man suits. The sky flashes red over their heads. Down the line everything comes to nothing. How we struggle today to make something of it. Such fools, we, such loving, living fools. I am partial to that which connects me to myself.

Being a nobody, nothing suits me quite well.

A SMALL BIT OF NOISE ON MY KNUCKLE

When Kate returned from the store with a full box of scars, I asked her what she intended to do next. "Count my wounds," she said, "and apply labels to them." Time passed. I grew accustomed to the fact that Kate wore her pain in the form of an assortment of latex stick-ons.

She eventually discovered that the number of wrongs inflicted on her person was finite. She was happy to see that plenty of scars remained in the box to use as spares, should one of the old scars fall off, or for emergencies, should a new scar be needed to label a new wound.

"Darling," I said one night, "You look wonderful." I meant what I said. We should all be so honest with our pain.

A TEXTBOOK'S SHIMMY
IN A CARPENTER'S BIND

The longest screw in the world is screwed into my wall. I am taking a moment out of my unscrewing to catch my breath. "Still at it?" my wife says, goes on with her life. I nod. Another year gone. Another gray hair falls to the floor. The mice sweep them into piles and run them through their mouths to use as spittle-stiffened swords. They duel with one another at my feet.

I gave up ambition long ago, long before ambition quits the ordinary man. Decades ago, I said: "That screw had got to go." Decades later, it is still going, still coming out of the wall. "I never knew," I say to my wife when she shuffles by, "that a screw could be so long, a wall so thick."

She is tired of hearing it, but I am afraid to tell her anything new about the screw. Each day, I know that when I reach the screw's end and extract it from the wall with a proud grin, the hole it leaves behind will be my grave, and that no wife wants to hear such talk in the middle of an otherwise fine day. I am close now, oh so very close to the end.

YEAST

Capable of becoming any one of the world's creatures, a magic yeast became a man and drank beer for the first time.

Magic yeast, unknowing cannibal.

WITH OUR MOLARS

Take aim, take aim! At targets we will shoot. Ashoot, ashoot, ashoot! A kick in the ass with a sooty, with a snooty, with a boot. Out with it, out with it! Out it goes, outing, outing, pulled with pliers through the nose.

We'll go anosing, anosing, knocking around our woes. We'll burn them, burn them, make diamonds out of coals! I swear it, I swear it, I plan to make my life interesting. Livid, livid, livid, from the tool shed to the bed.

We're hammering! We're nailing! We're screwing, building the end! Here it comes, crashing down! Crashing, acashing, cashing in. That was just the beginning.

Who cares what you think! You stink! You stink!

TIRED OF RUST AND BROKEN BONES

Listening to the rain is enough tonight where the moon has left the sky a cloud-filled pasture of mirrors.

The true work of the world goes undetected by the minions of gravel-toting laborers while bees grant honey to the blind.

In the morning, a single bee will mistake the hole in your den's unpatched screen for a possible entrance into new comb.

You will have to capture it in an empty glass to release back into the world of dew and criss-crossed sagging lines.

In the way of meaning stands a subtle blend of whiskey-stained aggravation and clocks passing through windows without breaking.

A CHIME FOR HIS ACHE

Painters almost captured its haze. Dolphins sang sad songs about curiosity. A terrible thing was said by someone in the back row. The red velvet curtain fell through the stage.

At last there had been a breakthrough of encouragement, little crowds of pale birds around the body.

THE DEAD KLIMT, 1917

The phones tonight are filled with drowning sleepless souls. There are shadows on the wall, docks to work at, muscles to build.

The wasp sleeps in a blue fabric's fold, but its secret is not mine. There are openings for an assistant, hearts bent double to serious places.

Blurred wanderings and jackboots stomp down cobblestoned Paris streets, while old women walk behind the parade, sweeping.

Sleep continues to evolve dreams out of unspun false cotton, while a grinning gray horse smiles through glowing green eyes.

There are patches of sunlight where the scars once stood, and even the milkman has interrupted the worry of his route to look.

THE CAREFUL FOREST

Floating cows were tethered to each tree marked for eviction. Blue pitchers filled with rain water sat on a table of melting ice.

A teary-eyed doe licked sweat from my hand. I reached for a pair of scissors. Seven men with trumpets raised their horns and played.

I cut the cow tethers free from their trees. Replacing clouds with cows, think of it!

DESNOS IS HERE TONIGHT

For a few sheaves of stolen light, an illuminated crowd spoke no tongue and chose to hang one of its own, a priest, who licked his lips and asked that his cheeks be rouged before the stringing, and would it be too ridiculous to wear a clay parrot while climbing the stairs to the platform.

At the top, he turned to the crowd and waved. No mask for the priest, no black sock of blindness. The noose was made of the finest silk, woven in India by a man later mauled by tigers. The priest declined a cigarette but requested a moment of silence to watch a flock of birds circle around the tower where his last night was spent.

A blind man pushed his way to the front and heard it as it snapped, the scent of broken neck, the flutter and flap of wings turned south. The priest's body dangled as the birds found purpose and became something raindrop-like without touching the ground.

A STEAM SCREEN OF HEARTS

My window implied that it wanted something from me. I checked to see that the moon was still in the sky. I closed my window's mouth. An elk stood outside the sill, fogging the glass with its breath.

I was resolute, I did not give in. I did not draw circles in the pane. My fingers are pure, and I have finally convinced myself that the elk is smarter than my window.

SHIN RUBBLE

Nothing has settled well, not my stomach, not the dust of broken bones. The house built for me by the emperor sags beneath the weight of his architect's royal lines.

My feet rove across muddy grounds, my eyes are ridiculed by the finding of four-leaf clover.

Something has touched my spine, a bead of icy water or the wrist of a red velvet curtain.

WRITTEN BY ONE OF THE CHORUS

I walked out of the desert with a brick and a chicken. In the shade of my oasis palm I brained the bird and built a small house of stone. There was honey in the cheese and doubt in the foundation.

Souls never early or late, we ate well before sleeping on my new stone floor.

FACES IN THE ROCK FACES

I saw a gnome in some rough by the side of the road. He saw me and waved. Our bus kept going. I dreamed that we had arrived, but when I woke we were still in the middle of nowhere.

I read my passport. It said that I had never arrived, but in my picture I am smiling.

ANOTHER WORD FOR PILGRIM

The shaman's veil swept across my feet. Inconclusive evidence about muskrat poaching is projected onto the screen. I am sad. I understand those deranged images.

The world is explained to me when a train gets lost on its way to a wedding.

NOTES OF A KIN-CANNED MAN

Seated in this corner, my back is to the tree. It reminds me of the woman upstairs whose sewing machine reminds me of an old dog backed into a couch's corner.

I count the hairs on my head and pass the time waiting for my refugee woman to call and tell me more stories about the chestnuts found in the pockets of Hungary's fugitive trees.

THE NET

I caught something in my net. I didn't know what it was, but I liked it all the same. I didn't know what to call it, so I called it Something.

Then one day I lost it. Did I miss it when it was gone? Yes, I missed it, even though I never knew its real name. Maybe it was Nothing.

SLOW CHILDREN

There are slow children in my neighborhood, but I never see them. Maybe they move so slow that they are invisible to the naked eye. In the sign's depiction of the slow child, though, he is running.

Maybe the slow child has yet to arrive, maybe that's him, that dust mote smeared like a question mark on the horizon.

SO MANY WHEELS AND SO MANY GALLOWS

Whatever it was, you can't find your way back without it. No maps mark those shores, no signs spare your guess, as if you are not supposed to know that a stranger found it while combing the beach for black pearls and turtle eggs.

It isn't that you want it back—you don't—but that you want to remember what it was, because you can't. And if the stranger claimed it as his own, would you want him to keep it or toss it back to the green sea, where such missing links thrive like diamonds on widowed rings.

BIRDS THAT ARE BLUE IN THE AIR

It is not your absence that is unpleasant, nor your final lack of presence, but my reluctant acceptance of the fact that you never appeared.

What test measures one's strength against one's tolerance? Roots of the medieval dwell in the stodginess of those unable to imbibe the virtue of immorality.

When pockets of trust exist in the land, there is premature relativity. A sap is worse than a rabid dog's bite. She seems to look, but our eyes meet without locking.

Her face is filled with doors, but behind none of them is the hand that will tear at cloth, the lip that will kiss and bleed.

SO IT GOES

What mottled bones are these that juice the mirrored knees of my sometimes constant wish? At last there is envy, painted in such lusterless swirls that all tact has been removed.

If you'd listen I'd fall asleep and satisfy your need for silence. What follows is only a rehearsal for the main song. In blood there is laughter, reason to smile without cracking teeth.

As if stamped adhesions were all you digested, I mailed letter after letter. Dust fell without reception. Unopened, my correspondence flew back to perch. Without resonance, echoes went unsounded.

I found wasting away necessary to produce the coded text that might retrieve your leavings. Yellowed newspaper clippings were yesterday's rote. "You live once," she whispered, "why do anything twice?" We were at it again before nightfall.

I possess a drunken craving for sobriety, but gin will do just fine.

SUNDAY'S BEST

"You goat," she said. "Can't you see my wings?" I saw her wings, but not the distance between us. "Kiss me," I said. She flew away.

A bird will never kiss a goat, it will only pick at the nape of its neck.

TRESTLE

I see her everywhere. She paints clocks without hands. Is that her impression of me? I need a small room to find relief.

There are warts on the bottom of my table, a difficult situation.

ACCIDENTAL SHARPS AND FLATS

Be brave, show me how strange you are. Like eggs, or insects when they hatch, skeletal psychosis rubbing its leg against coarse terrain, waiting to find the dream that unpeels rind. Run to the red purse, walk back to friends, catch an orange.

You looked at me from the edges. I will center you and throw a pot.

INSIDE A RING

Like the breath of a dying horseshoe crab, I've lost my
tongue to the aqualight.

NIGHT CROSSING

Something about a day that resembles a dream: the familiarity of a strange place, a new voice, recognition of possibility, coming to life. At the same time, it's in a brown paper bag. It might have been a sandwich, it might have been a wish.

Starting from top to bottom, the middle yields more than just a middle. A hole is everything the middle is not.

CLUSTER

Satellite encrusted with barnacles.   Skin of hyperspace, glowing coal, the butt of a gun pointed at a tug boat, reason to believe a revolution will arrive.

(Sad eve of a happier day...)

COMBINE

Cracked glick of frog glitch. Pond, term of confine, over-boiled, soaked in resin, reason for warrant. A can't is a not that didn't rant.

(Waiting for spoons to bend...)

RAIN

Rain fell on the roof of my car. Fingers drummed on the hood of my future wreck. I leaned over for a first kiss.

Tap Tap, the rain said, more is on its way.

UNLIKE LIFE

No resurrection, no flowers beyond the grave, but no reason to weep or wreck a life thinking about it. Isn't once just enough to play your few or only cards?

Between the first and final act a work of art, surrounded by the living, dying for a part.

THE CLICK OF THE ELECTRIC CLOCK

There! I had a poem, but lost it in a blur of words, except to say, which reminds me, I underlined my favorites, the lines that struck me, made me gasp or laugh in all those books I read, to remember for myself what I have seen and where I have been.

I was there, yes, and here too, a rare breed with a distinct instinct for extinction.

TWO FOR SOUPAULT

WHEN THE MOON EATS AT THE TABLE

No more. I need to piss. The snow ploughs, too often a
reflection and green light and automatically becoming an
Escher-like image in the knob.

Silver in your eyes I dream of biting. It's inside out. You
weren't at the recital. I left. No more waiting.

FEAR IS A MADWOMAN

Idiots. One more log to list. Green bag at the top of the
stairs, inconsiderate voices no concern.

Having drawn the blank card, the check flies bad. Your
hope melts. I'm unlisted but you'll find it.

In melting there is luxury. The can without label, the table
with paper, the clock. Idiots never die.

1/2 SURREALISM

Soupault is dead. The song is middled out and I'm insane without knowing I know grief.

In the morning come new groups of words, herds stampede, branches to pick like tears on frozen strings.

WINE

This string of wine, a pearl that falls without explanation. At last we have found a path that leads to charged forks.

Our options are wide to be brought forward in glazed meadows. This thing that did not exist now does.

MUSEUM

I want to know your silver-ringed hands, that look of laughter and curiosity in your eyes. You are a most precious and beautiful work of art.

I am sad that you will remain so until the last veil has been drawn shut and curtained, the museum closed.

IMAGINE

Imagine a dawn much like this one except you are not alone in the room. I have risen for a glass of water and watch you sleep as I drink and listen to the rain outside. How safe that time will be.

The birds have sung a reminder suggestive of future perfections while spiders make ready to sustain a similar length of strange rope. That dawn will come.

UNAVOIDABLE

I was staring out a window--there were three clouds in the sky. They followed the wind (or did the wind push them forward, towards some understanding of what they were meant to be--rain cloud, shade, or a poet's imagery?).

This is why when I see you again and again at different points in time and different points of the compass I wonder if I am following you or if you are following me, and I realize there is only one way of knowing if the unavoidable wind is blowing us two clouds into the moment's periphery.

We're moving along the horizon, two slow elephants in an unavoidable wind: do you want to follow it with me?

SUMMER CORN

A certain version splayed the self, a summer flayed, laid out for eyes to bare. Unbared, she bared her own, steeped towards promise.

Desire waits patiently, called on for pandemonium, for secrets to be revealed, lowered to uncoveted mask, a dance of sick venal sick-Ness, less its monster, come to feed, come to drink, Amherst carriage wheels to evening shrink.

Bounced on barber's ruts, cosmetic opium ruts.... Here stands to reveal, there to conceal. Soon the ring toss expands, ungrips moss, reverses the down-turned force.
An eye, my eye, watches over me, over broken barrels. Here, we've uncorked life, a party, come to drink, shirk your responsibilities.

(Summer people assembling to assault, adapt, adore the wretched tedium. Here we count hours, not days, of unlinked revulsion. Silent, green, the blank canvas unfurled for rippling winds, hot winds, hot breath…

Here we have a truth, a single speakable truth—the hot breath of summer, in my ear, in your ear.)

DECEMBER 14, 1914

I've looked for mystical illumination, found only page after page of moldy damp.

The awning that tugs the initiate forward conceals a lawn of crowded hopeless hope.

The painting's frame is flaking gold leaf. Its canvas is scratched enough to reveal a second and third painting beneath the first:

An idyllic study of the countryside, a portrait of a man on his knees, covered finally by nine amber bottles surrounded by oranges, lemons, and grapes.

Three different styles and three different eyes, three painters known only to have lived and died.

THE FIVE BASIC TYPES OF MISERY

I sat and watched it snow, my thoughts as empty as the space between the flakes. I read of your death. It must have been a terrible thing, but now I'm happy that you're well.

I've stared out at the same landscape for hours, but it is me that changes, not it, as the lines are buried. I wanted to tell you something, that none of it can be put into words, that words aren't good enough for it.

I've consumed many books since you went. None of them lives up to the time we spent shivering beneath the blankets. I was given a message to pass along, but it has since been intercepted, and I don't seem able to remember a thing.

GREEN GRASS

An orange sun sets in your eye's crate. Dead languages lost at sea, we are in a ship on a Viking raid, looking for words to bring back to the shores of our new world. Dried blood spilled on our leathers, a new language's worth of wounds, funeral pyres were sent out to sea.

Navigating our way home by the stars, we dreamed of land and hot food. Beneath quilts in the silence of night, we shared our stories. This scar, I said, was accidental. A clean wound on a cold beach, I slipped and fell on my sword, and there as I bled, a map of the *known* world lay before me with an X to mark our hut.

You were sleeping when I first tempted death. Now, we lay awake, breathing to pink sunrise. Your fingers trace a water's wake across the scar. You make a wish, that red rise to sunrise light without blood, that blood course through veins to a day when the spring draws us closer to its source, away from the source of longing, and towards the farthest pinnacle-neck of land.

There, on that distant beach, with the loss of loss between us, gain of gambled hope behind, satisfied to have sought and found a wind to lead us both astray, the gull our book of songs, on that lonely beach we will build a house. Stacked rocks will hold the sound of dead voices. Caught in mid-scream, these bricks, when broken open, will peal a toll's wealth of words.

They will scramble to undam the back of our throats, where dry pipes dream of tiger monks, a chest's drawn lunge, claxon-shorn walls on fields of staircase flowers.

TWO: FRAGMENTS

THE OLD MAN

The air was pure and clean in that part of the room, so I stayed there and watched the magnesium light flicker in my eyes and on the walls, and sometimes I listened to the feral machines coming out of the radio, black as licorice, sick as loveless breath, shivering not from cold or fear, but in disgust. The Old Man stood in the opposite corner of the room. I told him to stay put there and I'd bring him food, or something might swing that door open suddenly and break his nose. He stood there glaring at me. It was the first time I'd really looked at him and I still couldn't describe exactly what he looked like.

The magnesium sparks falling from his eyes were so bright, I could never quite get through the waterfall to find the secret caves in the sockets where all the plumbing was kept. He disappeared, now and then, I could see that, and then all I could see was the hospital's empty corridor and the doctor coming out of a door at the end of the hall, and from where I sat I could see in his eyes that the evil shined so bright and that he was going to shake his head and tell me she was dead, and I'd sit there like that forever until the corridor faded and made way for the garden, where I grew my own vegetables for summer salads and sat alone at a rust-colored picnic table listening to the crickets and grasshoppers and the swoosh of wind in the fields, the sigh of the breeze as it breathed life into the leaves of all the trees and the emerald dress I first saw her in.

"Some day you're going to like me," I said one day after I'd known her for about a month and wanted to find out For Real-For Real if she liked me or not, and we went on a tour of the beer factory together and listened to the shoosh of the amber as it flowed through the pipes. She was liking me better and better then, and I was running along the edge of one of her dimples, worshipping the rise and fall of her cheek and the welcoming blue-gray-green of her eyes. There was a place in the forest for the two of us to lie down together, on a bed of pine needles.

We gravitated towards the blue people, the friendly flame wraiths who lit our corn cob pipes and watched us run in the grass. "Woman, are you still alive?" I said to the night. I had just read her name in the sentence of a story that said she "died an hour ago up at the hotel." I cried and prayed to the sky outside. I heard her voice say she loved me and that she wanted me to say I loved her. She was moving away from me, across the green bridge. "What was she doing?" I asked The Old Man. "Just walking," he said. "A tree fell in a storm and hit her on the head."

I avoided the magnesium flare of his gaze by looking at the television patterns on his steel wool gloves. At first, I thought I was dreaming. Then I thought she was dreaming, and I'd traveled through time and found myself in her bed, awake in the middle of the night, not moving, not speaking, just arms wrapped around each other, watching the ceiling constellations spin and spiral. We floated through space together on our mattress, faces pressed against the glass, tracing dreams like skywriting in the clouds.

At first I was afraid it was only temporary, that I would never live by her side, but shadowy spindled things danced in my eyes and led me to a side room where mirrors were all reversed into the future. I was allowed to look just once, and saw us together on the side of a hill. It would be the first and last summer we'd spend together, but we made it last. Everything was green and blue and cloud-white and tickled us with a gentle breeze, unlike this long and lonely winter now scratching its toenails against the window where wasps built a nest when it was still warm. That summer ended with the tips of cattails bobbing in the breeze, an empty white rowboat floating downstream while we sat in the ferns by the shore.

Tonight the wind roars louder and louder through shivering trees. Somewhere the yard rabbit sleeps alone with a rocky stripe down the middle of her soul. She is the turtle walking lightly through my mind, the eggshell voice, the tail of a black comet streaking unseen through the night.

THE TARP

The Tarp was like an old scarecrow in a dusty black suit. Sometimes you could see him dancing on the lip of Pumpkin Hill, when the dwarves came out of their trailers to hunt.

"What are you hunting for?" The Tarp yelled down one night from his perch in the crook of The Evil Tree.

The Evil Tree was a petrified fork pointing up into the sky, the color of bone and just as hard. For a mile in every direction, the ground surrounding The Evil Tree was barren. One of the dwarves, a juggler, gave The Tarp his wicked eye and shouted, "You know better, Tarp, than to ask questions like that."

When he had disappeared behind the bowl head of the hill, The Tarp swung down from The Evil Tree's arm and began his dance. From a distance, he looked like a puppet in shadow against the scrim of a traveling Punch and Judy show's wagon.

I tried to keep him at a distance like that whenever I went out to hunt. As curious as I was to learn his secret, I had no interest in him learning mine, because I knew that if he took one look at my eyes he would know for sure, and that that was a price I was not willing to pay.

Nothing bad ever happened to me in the graveyard. When I was in grade school, we used to go there to smoke cigarettes or a joint before, during, or after class.

I can remember the perfect mushroom cloud of an exploded M-80 we set off one day, the way it rose up twenty or thirty feet into the sky above the expressionless faces of the headstones. Sometimes we'd rummage through the piles of flowers and wreaths in the cemetery's dump.

We stuffed our pockets with the cards that had the names of the dead stencilled onto them in black ink and later, before walking back to school, we'd pin them to our shirts and walk in a line with handfuls of old funeral flowers pressed between mock praying hands.

The alkaline gaze of Tarp's wandering eye, the phosphorous glow of his glass wand, the white light bleating from his electric teeth, the sad tone of his wolf cluck in the night, the padding feet of his wild dogs eyes red the color of steak blood mixed with the gray of bone and gristle; his dogs off at a flash of his silent whistle, The Tarp himself suddenly nowhere to be found.

There on the horizon in one moment and, in the next, off at a galloping lope to catch his chariot, pulled by two of Old Doc Maw's white mares set to running scared when one of the dwarves fired for fun into the sky at the eye of an unblinking bright full moon.

Their horseshoe cobblestone clop clops echoed against the hills and the trees and the pots and pans hung to dry near our cooking fire, whispering and cracking in the breeze like The Tarp's softly spoken "checkmate" every time he won a game.

HOUSE OF SLOTH

No, Minerva, the soil is not as rich and brown as we expected it would be, but the greens are greener and the longest days are longer than those on the other side. Did you think we'd be able to buy Paradise for next to nothing? This is the way we flog the beast: we tame it by killing it, we drown it so deep in our sorrow that we have no choice but to light the final fuse and blow. You remember those rooms we had to escape to find ourselves here, those word boxes of the dead who danced and sweated against one another, the deadness in their eyes disguised as life? How many times did we escape the crowd without scars, only to find ourselves vomiting in the cornfields? How many times did we make love with the sun coming up, our shoes still wet and sticky with the mud and muck of our night's overindulgence? We were stronger then than we are now, strong enough to do it two nights in a row, to kill ourselves one night and live to do it again the next, strong enough to rise and laugh about it and begin again with the morning sun.

The chickens are the ones that run around with their heads cut off. We are smart enough to just lay down and die when the time comes. Why do you count the hens each morning, when we've yet to see a fox, yet to hear a coyote howl? The only claws here are the fingers we sink into each other's backs at night.

When I'm coming home with the sunset at my back, I like to see your dresses drying on the line, swaying a slow dance in the breeze. I like it when the dinner bell rings, and it's just me coming in from the fields, just me coming from me to you.

Do you remember the face of that old man we talked to in the park? He must be long dead by now, asleep in his grave. I can only remember his face, and that what he said to us was so sad because we knew one day his words would become our truth. Sometimes I feel like we're sinking into quicksand, like you and I are holding onto a vine that's about to snap and no one's there to throw us a rope. That's why I just want to hold onto you now, that's why I just want to hold on.

I smile every morning when the pipes clank and clatter, and you wrap the pillow around your head, knowing it won't be enough to block out the sound, and I wrap myself around you and we lay like that for another hour.

I listen to you breathe, I feel your pulse next to mine as you hypnotize me back to sleep, and sometimes I get scared when the empty spaces between your breaths are so long and so empty. My stomach tightens and I nudge you to open your eyes and look at me and smile, and I know that we don't have to play games with each other, ever, because it's just us and the dusty roads and the fields and the stars.

It's raining now and I'm cold sitting here next to the window. You look so warm laying there, so content, and I'll be crawling under the covers to be with you for awhile longer before the coop starts to cackle and the sun begins to churn in the sky. But first I want to finish writing this and remember what I have written after I place the pages gently beneath the log that will soon burn as our morning fire.

NEIGHBOR

The day was cold and gray like today, which is probably why I remember you said that you wanted a fire to sit by where you could rub your hands and sip mulled wine through a cinnamon stick. Every night, you noticed, seemed to grow longer as the days died in their youth, and you began to wonder whether our supply of logs would live through the dead of winter, or if we'd be forced to snowshoe over to Milligan's with the sled to beg a half-cord to last us until spring.

You were stewing something in the pot, soup or stew, when we heard the crunch of snow outside the door, followed by the knock. Was it Milligan's youngest girl, or one of the twins? It's hard for me to remember because I was still under the covers, half asleep with a book, and all I heard, as if in a dream, was an anxious child's voice say, "Stillborn, won't you come? Paps said find the healer, Mam's going cold, bring the fire..."

You were packing your bag with things from the shelf, jars and pouches, herbs and ointments, and you had your boots on and were on your way to the door when it finally hit me what you were about to do. I slapped my book shut without marking the page and pushed the blanket off. My first step from the bed was onto one of your glass beads, and the little girl bolted down the path and stood with her arms around the neck of one of the dogs.

You laughed and said you wouldn't be gone long, maybe until morning, and I asked you what the hell you thought you were doing, Milligan was nothing but a fool and a ferret and a shotgun for brains neighbor all along, and you said, "Gonna help me with the pack, or get back into bed?" One of the dogs howled.

I looked through the frosted glass at Milligan's little girl, but I still couldn't see her face, she was already lining the dogs up on the rope. "Cow or child, ask her!" I yelled from the stoop, pulling my boots on. You yelled over your shoulder as the pack pulled away that Milligan wasn't keen enough to plant a spring birth and that you can't count on a baby to be on time, and then you were around the curve and the dog's barking faded into the trees. It was only after I had strapped on my suspenders, laced my hood, and closed the door behind me that I realized shit, you left without waiting for me or waving goodbye.

You didn't even know if that Mulligan woman was real; we'd never seen anything but offspring and Milligan's mean scowl which looked to me like the sullen face of a wifeless father, and there you went down the hill, one of the little Milligans in tow, the sky above looking down and thinking to drop more snow.

I coughed, but it wasn't because there was a spot of blood in the phlegm I spit into the snow that I went back for the shotgun, and it wasn't because I thought you had left without thinking twice that I strapped on the snowshoes. It wasn't because I felt immediately alone without you and the dogs and the stirring of the stove pot that I took down a bottle of whiskey for good measure.

It wasn't because I had a premonition of something bad about to happen that I set to tramping out in your tracks, but that when the blizzard's screen of snow began to fall, I wanted to be on the other side of it, backstage at Milligan's farm.

The others that come to you, I thought while trying to find the pace that would keep me close behind, come because they've still got something left to give, not because they've already lost it.

What can you do for a stillborn child, I thought, settling into my rhythm, and didn't bother to think that besides feeling like there might be something left for you to do for her, you were probably just as curious as I to find out what goes on inside a silent neighbor's house, and that it wasn't in the name of getting the goods that you set out as fast as you did, nor to exclude me from knowing, but because they had asked and you couldn't say no to someone who needed your help. But what made you think to cross the lake instead of going around it? It wasn't even a full day earlier that we'd decided the ice was too thin to fish through, and yet there were the tracks of the dogs and the sled pointing like a straight arrow towards the opposite shore and Milligan's place beyond. From where I stood, I couldn't tell if you'd made it across. Snow fell, darkening the sky, and the wind picked up and blew the light dust into plumes and tiny white tornadoes.

Your tracks disappeared ahead of me into a white cloud.

A THORNY TARMAC OF BRAMBLES

I have always lived near the river. Every morning at six a.m., the writer walks past my house. I don't remember the first time I noticed him. It isn't until someone passes in front of your eyes several times that you begin to recognize him or her as one of those strangers you never meet but always see. It was easy to mark the man who took his walks next to the river each morning as a writer.

There was something in his walk, the way he stooped forward and looked at the ground as he advanced, the mock seriousness covering his face with a satiric overlay of deep wisdom, the sardonic suggestion of infinite knowledge. I know by looking at him that he knows many things and that he recognizes the absurdity of our day to day plight called existence. I know by looking at him that he is superior to the common man.

Many people walk next to the river. From my window, I am able to see them without being seen myself. The writer also watches the people he encounters as they cross his path. His eyes move from ground to a face, to another face, then to the river or a girl on the street or an open window on the third floor of an interesting old house before returning to the ground again, where I imagine his mind visualizes pages of words spilling from the end of his pen about the people he has just seen and their lives he understands just by looking at them.

I have never left my house to follow the writer in his wake of thoughts, but one day, when my strength returns, I will. I'm sure that after he passes by, he must cross the third or fourth bridge and, at a corner table in one of those cafes on the opposite bank, begin his day's work.

It did cross my mind once that perhaps the man I thought to be a writer might turn out to be one of the criminally insane, since there are also lunatics who walk next to the river on their way to and from the nearby asylum. My suspicion embarrassed me, though. I felt shame for doubting my writer's veracity. I wished him the best and hoped for him to sell some of his work soon so that he might replace the shabby coat he's worn through two winters.

It is comforting to know that a writer walks past my house every day. It is reassuring to know that my house and my window are part of his day's landscape and that, after a morning when I am well enough to lean out over the balcony for him to see, maybe one day he will write a page about me.

MOON, COLD, AND CAT

I felt as if I was on celluloid. The icy gray of the moon, the sting of cold against my face, the sound of my footsteps on the crunchy snow, the taste of blood in my mouth, the smell of more snow on its way... The moon was bright. I was hit in the face by a snowball, no, it was my brother's fist. I had left the movie theatre after seeing a film that failed to move me. My brother and his wife were standing beneath a tree on the other side of the street. I crossed over to see them.

The trees in that part of the park were strung with white lights. I grabbed my brother by the collar and spun him round. I tried to throw him against a tree, but he grabbed onto my coat and tried to throw me to the ground. I swung my arm at his stomach. He blocked my punch and hit my forehead with his forearm. I stumbled backwards. He and his wife laughed. I felt my head throb as my face flushed red with embarrassment. I turned and walked away.

My brother and his wife were kissing. I stood several hundred feet away and watched them from behind a tree. Their arms were wrapped around each other. I thought about the day before, when I hugged a tree that looked lonely. It made me feel better, much better. I chose that moment in my thoughts to bolt. I ran towards them as fast as I could run with my face thrust forward, so that my jaw stuck out at a dangerous angle.

They turned their heads and saw me coming, pushed away from each other, one going left, the other right. I followed my brother, who ran screaming through the park beneath the trees. I ran behind him and screamed too. We were laughing. I wondered if he would ever stop running, because at that moment, I felt like I could not run any more, even though I knew my brother would tire first and that I would be able to catch him if I only stayed close. I heard him gasp.

He stopped running and turned towards me. He was laughing and gasping for breath. I lifted my black bag filled with heavy books and swung it at his body. He stepped back, but the bag hit him in the arm. He yelled out in pain, but continued to laugh. I swung again and missed. He stepped back. I stepped forward and pushed him to the ground. He held his hands over his face. I raised my bag and brought it down hard against the ground next to his head.

I swung again, and in that moment, as the bag came falling down, I knew that the moon was behind me, and that when my brother looked up, he would see the moon as a halo around my head and me as a white stallion reared up on its hind legs, my hooves about to crush his skull into a soft hollow of blood and bone.

"Enough is enough," my brother's wife said. I laughed and helped my brother up from the ground. The three of us walked slowly to the tree lit by white lights. I kissed my brother's wife on the cheek, shook my brother's hand, and left the park. I looked back and saw the two of them kissing. The icy white moon was shining down on me. Its light cast my shadow onto the snowy ground, where shivering cats drew circles around my feet, begging to be taken home for the night.

WHITE PAGES ON A BLACK SHELF

I left the milk factory and walked through the main gate to the street. I crossed the crosswalk, making sure to step only on the black stripes of the asphalt. There is already too much white in my life. At the end of the workday, I try my best to avoid it. It is said in my family that only the truly blessed child will bite at its mother's nipple while in suck and that the unlucky ones merely drink the milk. But I digress.

I bought a newspaper at the corner and continued on in the direction of the concert hall, where I was supposed to meet my wife, who works in the glue factory. As I walked and read the headlines, I heard a cough and looked up to find myself in the path of a man walking towards me. A collision seemed to be the next obvious event, but instead we stopped face to face, toe to toe, and looked into each other's eyes.

I immediately looked away and noticed, on the other side of the street, a pair of women in a similar position. I looked behind me to find similar configurations all the way down to the corner. Every ten feet or so, two people stood face to face. There were pairs of men, or one man and one woman, or two women. No children, though. A minute passed. Since, at the milk factory, there is nothing except predictable monotony, I remained still in the position that I found myself and concentrated only on the space in front of me, as if I was watching the bottles go by on the belt.

I began to think of my poor mother, who died when I was an. infant. My grandmother, who raised me, always said that it was bad luck to die and worse luck to live. I began to study the man's face. It was an average face, nothing extraordinary, but since I rarely take the time to look at faces, other than mine in the mirror and my wife's at the kitchen table, it occurred to me that I ought to study this particular face well, since I might be stuck with it for awhile. The man, in the meantime, continued to look at my eyes, even as they drifted from pore to pore, my scars, whiskers, and moles. Five minutes passed like this.

I began to think that I might never make it to the concert hall on time to meet my wife, but then, as if by some invisible sign, the man stepped aside and continued on his way. I looked up and down the street and saw that all of the pairs had broken up and that one member of each pair was left standing for a moment before moving on, perhaps like myself, wondering what it was all about.

My wife and I arrived from opposite directions at the same time in front of the concert hall. We both apologized for being late and walked, arm in arm, to the box office. I wondered, but didn't ask, if anything strange had happened to her that day.

We went inside.

VIOLENT REVOLUTION

The violent action happened so fast as to be a mere blur focusing itself at the back of his eye where it transmuted into electrical impulse spawned images registering a response somewhere in his mind while reminding him that what he had witnessed was real and deranged. The act, however, remained, and it was only through a process of elimination that he was able to untangle himself from his train of thought and walk away from the scene of the crime.

An outstretched hand grabbed his wrist while a voice screamed into his ear to go get help. But he was deaf to this plea and walked on, the hand detaching itself, the voice seeking another listener. In a moment he was getting into a taxi telling the driver where to go while looking through the cab's rear window at the crowd that was forming around the victim. He sighed and wondered what kind of world it was he lived in and noticed that the department store where he frequently shopped had changed its name within the last two days. He felt as if certain things were escaping him but could not put a finger on what they were.

When he tried to piece together the events leading up to the violent action he only saw a face and a blur with the hand on his wrist and the voice in his ear. It was the shape of the face that intrigued him most now as he thought more about it, and he realized that it belonged to the body of a schoolteacher from his grade school years. Memories of this particular teacher flooded into his brain. Outstanding in his mind was the birthmark shaped like a small egg on the teacher's forehead. Secondary to his mind came the memory of the teacher carrying the child he had once been to the nurse as he screamed in pain after falling out of a tree during recess, whispering in his ear that everything was going to be all right. The memories dissolved as he pictured the blur that may have disrupted his former teacher's life.

Reality set in as he watched the crowd gathered around the fallen man grow smaller and smaller through the taxi's rear window until he could fit the scene with one eye squinted between his thumb and forefinger held a quarter inch apart. His lack of emotion puzzled him as he pondered his teacher's demise. His unwillingness to get involved in the situation seemed to have deeply-rooted psychological implications, or maybe it was just that he was late for a very important meeting and had finally achieved a state of mind in his life that enabled him to blot out the realities around him that might become distractions to his every day mode of behavior. It was all he could do to ignore the violent world around him and although he was sorry to feel so thoughtlessly distant from the demise of a man who had once taught him to read and write in the second grade, he hoped that he would be able to confront his own violent end with the same disinterestedness one assumes towards a television that is on in a room where one is engrossed in a fine piece of literature without distracting the eye to behold the lack of merit playing itself out in the colored patterns of the hypnotic electric box.

By the time he arrived at his destination he had immersed himself in the present and made the immediate past a fuzzy impossibility that could only have been a dream left over in his mind from the night before. When he got out of the taxi and paid his fare he was oblivious to the fact that he had arrived at the same place where he climbed into the taxi just minutes earlier.

He walked through the revolving doors of the hotel lobby, where he met his acquaintance and suggested that they retire to the bar where one could enjoy a well made hot rum cider and watch the races on a small screen placed next to the ashtray on each table.

When he was quite sure that the meeting was a success, he excused himself from the new client, walked again through the revolving doors and into the street, where he felt a mere blur focus itself on the tip of his mind's understanding of the moment during which he was aware of a vague sense of familiarity with what was going on around him.

I climbed to the top of an ivory tower, where a beautiful young ballerina sat waiting for me. I laughed out loud and said hello.

"Are you ready?" she asked.

"Ready as a willow." I said, kissing her lightly on the cheek.

"Don't muss the cake, dear," she said.

I noticed that I had smeared her mask a bit in one place near the corner of her mouth.

"Goodbye, missy," I said, and walked out onto the balcony.

A dwarf, wearing tuxedo, top hat, and white gloves, sat on a milking stool and fiddled with a Rubik's Cube.

"Impossible," he said when he noticed me standing there above him. "Such a tiny thing and so hard to master."

"Yes," I agreed, "But there is a formula. If you've given up, that is."

"Formulas," the dwarf said, "are for those who can't deal with fuzzy impossibilities. I'd rather be confused and questing than clear-headed and lifeless."

"Do you have my feather?" I asked. "I really must be getting on with it."

"Oh yes, my good man," he said. "Sorry to delay your descent with fuzzy impossibilities."

He handed me the feather, medium-sized, yellow, with streaks of blue in the quill.

"Well then, I'm off," I said.

I leaped from the balcony, letting go of the feather as I began my descent. Looking up as I fell down, I saw that the feather was still well above me and taking its time getting to the ground, which reminded me of a story I hadn't thought of in years.

I was at a resort, strolling along the boardwalk. It was summer and all the ladies wore white dresses and carried parasols to hide their faces from the harsh afternoon sun. Up ahead, there was a crowd gathered against the boardwalk's railing. People were trying to get down the narrow stairway to the beach. A woman screamed, not at the spectacle that everyone else was straining to get a glimpse of, but because a large splinter of wood had come off the old boardwalk railing and lodged itself deep in the palm of her hand.

Blood from the wound poured freely onto the ground and all over the front of her white dress. Part of the crowd formed a circle around the woman and watched her bleed. No one seemed intent on helping her. She stood there, screamed, and went on bleeding. The main spectacle, though, was on the beach. I pushed my way through the crowd until I had a clear view of what was going on.

A whale had beached itself sometime during the night and lay panting and gasping in the shallow pool of water formed by the continuous drippings of a drainpipe extended out over the sand from some unknown source. There was only enough water in the pool to support the whale's death. It was too far from the water to be dragged and was too big for any winch, hook, ladder, or crane that might be located in the vicinity of the resort to lift it.

Somehow I was pushed to the front of the crowd, where I had to struggle to keep from falling into the pool of water, the whale's grave. I was pushing an obese woman holding a handful of red licorice away from me to get some breathing room for myself when the crowd suddenly fell silent.

I turned my attention back to the pool. A man waded towards the dying whale. I recognized him to be a waiter from one of the nearby cafes. He had a pistol in his hand, a blank expression on his face.

He approached the whale and, without flinching or pausing to consider his actions, emptied the pistol into the whale's brain. It shuddered and heaved for a moment, slapped its giant tail fin once against the water, and died. The man shook his head and disappeared into the crowd.

Strange that I should remember that story while gravity attracted me towards the ground, but then, my job always reminds me of strange things. I pulled my rip cord and floated to the ground at the base of the ivory tower. The feather had touched ground before me. I hadn't even seen it fall past me on the way down.

"Almost, but not quite," The Professor said. I was soon climbing the ivory tower's steps for another try.

TRIESTE, 1949

When he came down out of the hills, the old man knew he would finish the race and that it didn't matter that no one would be at the line to greet him. All of the others had finished hours ago.

He coasted as he left the hills behind, and even though the final decline into the town was steep enough to propel him into the square, he braked and rode slowly to read the names of the racers that had been written in chalk on the road by those who had gathered to see their favorite cyclists pass. He knew all of the names and said them aloud as he rode over them, just as he read their names aloud in the newspapers when the big races in other countries were reported.

The old man sneezed when he crossed the finish line. He parked next to the fountain in the town square, removed his shoes and socks to dip his feet into the cold water. He thought about all of the faces that had cheered him on from the side of the road and how the faces had thinned out and grown fewer and fewer as it got dark and the people went into their houses thinking that the last racer had passed, not knowing that an old man was bringing up the rear of the pack long after the pack had crossed the finish line.

He thought about the beginning of the race, when he was momentarily a part of the pack, and he thought about the fallen cyclist he passed soon after the rider hit the ground, blood pouring from behind the man's knee, the kneecap dislodged from its place on the man's leg. He remembered when one of his sons had fallen from his little bicycle the first time he tried to ride, and how he had fallen no more after that initial encounter with the ground. He remembered his son laughing and coasting down the dirt road towards the sea as white sails rippled on the water.

The old man left his bicycle next to the fountain with his riding shoes, cap, and number that had been tied around his chest, and he walked barefoot to the train station. The train was waiting at the platform. He paid for his ticket and climbed up into the train's sleeping cabins. He ordered ham and cheese sandwiches from the porter and asked him to bring a bottle of champagne on ice.

"I've finished the race," the old man said to the porter when he brought in the bucket of ice for the champagne bottle he was holding in the crook of his arm while balancing the tray of sandwiches in the other hand. The porter smiled, asked the old man if he wanted anything else, and closed the sleeping cabin's door.

The old man was now alone with his sandwiches and champagne and he drank a toast to himself and the success of the race. He pulled down the bunk from the compartment's wall and climbed beneath the covers with a glass in one hand, bottle in the other, the sandwiches on his lap.

Sometime in the middle of the night, while the old man slept and the train sped towards Trieste, a street sweeper found the bicycle and the old man's things next to the fountain. He threw the shoes and cap and number into a bin and rode the bicycle home, where his son would soon be waking up to celebrate his eleventh birthday.

ON THE METRO

Once, while waiting for a bus to take them home after a night of wandering the streets and sitting in cafes, they stood in front of a costume shop's window display in which there were three funhouse mirrors. One made their heads large and their bodies small, the second made them look like dwarves, and the third altered their figures into what looked like thin stings of malleable rubber. They laughed at their grotesque reflections and waved their arms in the air. When the bus came, he had to pull her away from the window. She wanted to stay and play with her double. As the bus pulled away from the stop, she waved goodbye to the masks that stared out at the street from the window.

In the museum he walked slightly behind her to watch as she looked at the paintings and sculptures. He wondered what he saw with her eyes that he didn't see with his. He wondered if they could ever see anything the same way. After all the time they had spent together, she continued to surprise him. Sometimes, standing next to her, he felt as if she was far away, as if they were talking on the phone or through a thick cloud and not the candle's flame or the taste of wine. He wondered what it would be like to say he finally knew her, but he also knew that if he ever reached that point, they would no longer have any reason to live for each other.

On the metro, he sat across from her, next to an old woman returning home from the market. While she watched his face, he stared at his feet and played with the ring they found one day at the park. She smiled when she remembered digging her hand into the sand and coming up with the ring. She wondered what a wedding band would look like on his finger and how his eyes would look at hers when he leaned forward to kiss her. She pictured the two of them together in their hotel room after the wedding as he draped his coat over the back of a chair and turned to her.

The old woman was loaded down with bags of fresh bread, fruit, and vegetables. A bottle of wine clunked against a bottle of olive oil as the metro swayed and bounced along the tracks. The old woman was tired from the trip to the market and struggled to keep her eyes open and her head from nodding back against the window. He stared at his new black shoes, comparing their shine to the old woman's scuffed and muddy boots. He glanced across the aisle and wondered if they would live together long enough for him to see her feet grow old and veined like he imagined the old woman's feet to be.

The metro was soon crowded with people standing and pushing against one another. Few of them spoke. Most of stared at the floor or at the back of the person nearest them. Some looked blankly through the metro's windows into the darkness of the tunnel. Some used the window to stare at the other passengers. She could not see his face. Strangers were standing between them. She began to imagine that she was alone again, that the hand she had been holding earlier belonged to someone she never knew, but the next stop was theirs and interrupted her thoughts.

They stood up at the same time, left the car together, and climbed the stairs to the street, where they disappeared, hand in hand, into the same light.

A TIME OF PLATES

Rick is secretly jealous of Tom's possession of the plate. I must say that I myself am also jealous, but I try to remember that jealousy is a bad thing and that I was not forced to relinquish my ownership but gave it away freely. I also reminded myself that had I not given the plate away, had I not decided to share the plate with others, the plate would not exist. I brought the plate to life by circulating it, though now I wonder if I wasn't a bit premature with my generosity. Rick is jealous. I am jealous too. Tom is extremely satisfied.

When I returned from the bank with my money, I found my brother with his girlfriend. I could no longer tolerate the stares of those against the plate, and decided right there that the plate was a bad thing. "I no longer want this plate," I said to my brother, and placed it on the ground next to his feet. He looked at it and shook his head.

"Whatever, dude," he said, returning his attention to his girlfriend. I realized then that he neither cared for nor had any opinion whatsoever about the plate, and that there must be a third group of people, somewhere, made up of individuals with a viewpoint similar to my own. I leaned down, picked up the plate, and went to look for a sandwich.

A young man and woman passed in front of me. The woman was carrying a box, in which all manner of objects were seated. The man asked, "Why do you like this box?" Although the couple moved out of my hearing range before she gave an answer, I recognized the possibility that there existed a whole group of box people, and that the young woman who passed before me might have been carrying the Box Of All Boxes and that, possibly, with his question, the man was in the midst of trying to wrest possession of the box from she to him, just as Tom had manipulated the plate out of my hands and into his greedy grasp.

"That bastard," I thought. "Tom will have the plate forever. Rick said it would be so. But then, Rick wanted the plate for himself just as much as Tom."

What is one to do? We all need a panacea.

GIVING THANKS

As proscribed in The Tablet, first runic document to declare the law in our new land, I placed one of my belongings, a typewriter, outside my door on Sunday and left the house from noon to five.

I spent the afternoon wandering through the recently discovered labyrinths beneath the library, documenting for our new catalog the dates and titles of the dusty ancient volumes that will make up our humble institution's new wing.

When I returned home, the typewriter was gone, replaced by three paper bags, one filled with potatoes, one with apples, and one with pears.

"Pears!" I shouted with delight.

Every Sunday, our new government showers us with the fancies of our imaginations. I carried the bags into my house and returned to my terminal. It glowed with green vitality as I performed my calculations.

I was close to finishing the project that would enable our architects to calibrate the number of memorials and monuments to be installed over the next five years in relation to building expansion and projected population growth. Our builders want a consistent grid, fifty statues or plaques per square kilometer.

Next Sunday, I plan to leave an antique movie camera. It still works, but I don't have the money to pay for film. In exchange, I hope to receive a box of steaks. It's been months since I last had meat.

A CRATER FILLED WITH CAULIFLOWER

Placard has been placed under house arrest until the elders decide his case. He can continue to work his fields, but if he climbs a fence, if he breaches a wall, if his foot touches the road, we will shoot him, shoot him dead.

We have been given our orders, and we intend to execute them to the letter if Placard forces our hand. His dossier says that he poses no threat to the armed forces, but that he does have a keen mind and should not be bargained with.

There seems to be much confusion in town. The elders have sent a scout into the city to find out what's going on, and they continue to argue amongst themselves. With nothing else to do while they bicker, we watch Placard.

Some of the crack squad are hoping he makes a move, but the bets are running heavily in his favor. Life over Death. Placard waves to us from his tractor and we wave back. This morning we photographed him when he began to plant the heads.

"What are you planting?!" one of the privates yelled across the barricade.

"Corn!" Placard yelled with a smile.

Most of the squad laughed and prodded one another with their elbows or rifle butts. When the laughter died down, I leaned forward in the seat of my jeep to hear Placard's answer, but he only smiled and revved the tractor's engine. One of the men asked if he could return to town for some beer. I signed his orders and told him to bring a newspaper back with the keg.

Last week, Placard drove slowly through town after returning from the city with a wagon full of heads. When asked where he had purchased the heads and for how much, Placard just smiled and shook his head. There was much finger pointing and bickering between the elders. No one knew what to do, or what to think. The elders argued late into the night, and the tavern remained open a full two hours past its normal closing time.

Placard sat by himself in a corner booth. Some of the other farmers sent pints over to his table. These he accepted with a nod and a wink. There seemed to be some kind of silent understanding in the town that when the elders made their decision, it would be in everyone's best interest to be on Placard's good side. But no one approached him, and no one said anything to him.

At three in the morning, a courier came to my table with a note from the elders, asking me to place Placard under house arrest, an act which I promptly accomplished by informing Placard that he should, after finishing his final pint, return to his farm and stay there.

"How long will this last?" he asked.

"Until this matter with the heads has been cleared up," I told him.

"So," he said, burped, and left the tavern.

I radioed to base for the crack squad to be sent and followed Placard, at a distance, up to the gate of his farm. My squad arrived minutes later and took up positions around the perimeter of Placard's property.

A soft drizzle began to fall. In their tents, my men breathed deeply and began to snore. A light came on in one of the house's windows and immediately went dark, as if Placard's home had nodded at us, smiled, winked, and gone to sleep.

A tense standoff in the city has made it necessary for the outer provinces to be made to understand the grave consequences that will follow any more subversive acts such as Placard's transportation of human remains from city to village for agricultural purposes.

We have just been given our orders from Central Command: "Seize the heads."

We go in at dawn.

AT WORK IN THE AGITATION

"Apples don't fall from birch trees," I thought while walking home from town, but there it was, a perfect red apple on the ground, and a French woman had just smiled at me back at the corner. A red apple on the ground, a French woman's smile. "How are they related?" I wondered, and kept walking. Neither had caused me to interrupt my pace; I said hello to the woman and glanced at the apple. But then, immediately after my double encounter, both smile and apple brought questions into my mind. How did I know that the woman was French when she hadn't said anything to me? What did her smile mean? What was its cause and its intent? What would happen if I ate the apple or picked it up and put it in my coat pocket?

A block later, I stood on the bridge over our town's inconspicuous but proud little stream, unable to make myself cross to the other side. It wasn't that an invisible barrier had risen before me, but that my mind refused to allow me to go any further without contemplating the implications of the grounded apple beneath the birch tree. Many times I see strange things that take me out of my mundane train of thought and place me in an area of reflected pause, where it becomes necessary to understand the possible connections or meanings between random, or not so random, objects and events.

What was I thinking about before the French woman smiled at me? Nothing much, except that the Chinese restaurant I was coming from had become inconsistent in the preparation of their dishes and that it seemed odd that they didn't automatically supply fortune cookies at the end of the meal, but waited until you asked for them to bring the plate out. I thought about when the restaurant first opened, when the owner greeted guests at the door and walked from table to table smiling and making small talk.

He was an energetic man then, but perhaps it was only the rush of optimism supplied by the venture's first days that made him this way, because after that first week, he was slowly transformed into a different man, which turned the restaurant into a different restaurant. Where he was once animated and energetic, he now remained seated at a booth in the back, staring at the receipts laid out in front of him like tarot cards. And where the staff had once reflected the owner's cheer and amiability, they now mirrored his dark mood and only grunted when you made a selection from the menu. If the owner saw portents of the future in those receipts, he probably did not want to believe what his eyes were telling him.

That is what I was thinking, and then my mind went blank, as it often does after I have eaten and am enjoying the comfort of my full belly. I arrived at the corner. The French woman smiled at me. Was she waiting there for someone? Was she waiting there for me? I said hello and turned the corner. When I looked back, she was walking in the opposite direction, but turned to look at me again after she had crossed to the other side of the street. I saw her laugh just as I laughed. It is rare that you see a stranger on the street, make eye contact with them and, when you look back to see them going their way, find that they have looked back as well.

It was an awkward moment. Does one stop and wave? Does one walk up to them and start a conversation? Or, and this is what seems to happen most often, do you both look away, startled by the suddenness of the strange connection that has been made? In this instance, both of us looked away laughing and it seemed as if enough had happened between us, except that as I kept walking I wondered if perhaps she, the French woman who had smiled at me, was meant to be the connection I had until that moment, both consciously and unconsciously been waiting to appear for so long, and that now, by walking carelessly in the opposite direction without exploring the implications of our interaction, however fleeting, I might be forsaking the only chance at something real, something meant to happen specifically for me and only me.

I thought of the one other time I had turned to watch a woman walk away from me after making eye contact on the street. When I turned around, I found that she too had stopped to turn and look at me. We stood there, twenty feet apart, and looked at each other without smiling, without reacting in any way, as if seeing a painting or a statue for the first time before forming an opinion about it.

We stood like that for a full two minutes until, finally, she walked up to me, touched my cheek with a black leather-gloved hand, and said: "I'm sorry, I was hoping you were someone else, but you only look like him." "It's strange for me, too," I told her. "Your ideals?" she asked. "No," I said, "My instincts. Looking at someone and knowing." "Yes," she said. "It gets closer and closer without revealing itself. It's there, but it isn't. You hear only its echo, as it is already far away." I turned and continued on in the direction I had been walking, without stopping to look back again.

The way the apple had been placed on the ground next to the birch tree, or the way it had fallen, made it stand out from everything else: it was meant to be considered, whether or not someone had planned it like that. I looked at it and looked away, and kept walking. Until I stopped on the bridge, though, I was unable to equate the impression that the apple had made on me with a series of words that might allow me to welcome its implications into my life. As the water slowly trickled under the bridge, two things occurred to me simultaneously: one, that I had no idea where the stream led to or ended or turned into a river or a lake, and two, that eating the apple would kill me. I laughed at the nude absurdity of my second supposition, but knew, at the same time, that I was right.

I pushed my hands deep into the pockets of my coat and walked fast, my head lowered, eyes glued to the road in front of me, until I returned to the tree, saw the apple on the ground and the French woman standing next to it. She smiled at me when I returned. I stood next to her, removed my glove and slipped my bare hand into hers.

THE GARDEN PARTY

It was a lovely little garden party. Vanilla cakes and tea were being served and the ladies were hovering around the serving table, talking about the decorations, the cakes, the weather and the latest gossip. Mrs. Primly was being very careful about keeping her dainty white lace shoes clean. She remembered what had happened when she stepped in a puddle at another garden party years ago when she was much younger and much sillier.

She had ruined one of her lace shoes and was forced to listen to the other ladies as they shrieked with laughter at her faux pas. She was terribly embarrassed and blushed coyly as she wiped the shoe with her pink hanky. As she bent over, someone reached down and handed her a paper napkin.

"Use this dear," the woman said. "No need to ruin a perfectly wonderful handkerchief."

Mrs. Primly started at the sound of the voice she hadn't heard in years and looked up into the smiling face of her old acquaintance, Mrs. Wafer, who had gone away with her husband. The two women, surprised and startled to see each other, exchanged hugs and kisses on the cheek.

"Why, Mrs. Wafer, how many years has it been since I last saw you?" Mrs. Primly asked.

"Many years, Mrs. Primly, many years," said Mrs. Wafer.

"Do you remember Vera, Eva, and Barbara?" asked Mrs. Primly.

"Barbara is David's sister," said Mrs. Wafer. "Vera and Peter are at the theatre."

"Who is David?" asked Mrs. Primly.

"He is a Swede. His sister is called Zina. He is a poet. She is an economist."

"He speaks Czech?"

"He loves jurisprudence. We were at home all the time in July."

"George is a lawyer now," Mrs. Primly boasted about her oldest son.

"Who ate all the candies?" Mrs. Wafer asked.

"I drink only water," Mrs. Primly said.

"That is an echo," retorted Mrs. Wafer, with cruelty in her voice. "I love Southern nature, but L.V. charges so much."

"Yes, the price of things," Mrs. Primly responded. "Who is L.V.?"

"L.V. Scherba is a specialist in Russian grammar. A whole month now, and the cheek is still swollen. Ah, the price of the brush..."

Mrs. Primly looked at her old friend and asked: "A quotation from Cicero?"

"It's terribly hot today," replied Mrs. Wafer. "A hat would not keep out the sun."

"July was very hot," Mrs. Primly said.

"In the Sahara it is dry," stated Mrs. Wafer. "The elders should know better than to use yellow leather."

"What?" Mrs. Primly asked, trying to clear things up.

"Don't you listen anymore?" said Mrs. Wafer, raising her voice. Some of the other women looked over to see what was going on. "Everything is perfectly clear!" Mrs. Wafer said loudly.

"What?!" Mrs. Primly asked again, this time with an expression of confusion on her face. "I don't understand..."

"That is an echo!" shrieked Mrs. Wafer as she slapped Mrs. Primly across the face.

"Eggs don't teach the hen..." she added, and walked away, leaving a teary-eyed Mrs. Primly in a state of shock.

Her old friend had changed considerably. The strain of it all was almost too much for her to handle. As if coming out of a trance, Mrs. Primly realized that all the other women were laughing at her. She turned and screamed "Be Quiet!!!" but they went on laughing.

Without looking back, Mrs. Primly left the garden party.

TOEHOLD ON A SHEEP'S HEAD

It began to rain, so I closed the window, lit the candles, plugged in the Christmas lights and sat down to waterproof my shoes. I listened to love songs and pondered a black and white photograph of Charlotte Rampling I had taped to my wall. It was a good night for us to be together.

I picked out an old shirt I no longer wore from a pile of old shirts in the corner. I sat down on my bed and set about shining my shoes. Raindrops tapped lightly against the window. Somewhere behind the clouds, either dancing or napping, the full moon smiled. It was a beautiful night to be shining shoes. I applied mink oil to the leather and rubbed it in a circular motion. I noticed that the laces on both shoes were frayed and that each tongue beneath the lace was wrinkled and cracked.

I heard voices outside. I looked out the window at the street below. A group of four women were wet and laughing about how wet they were as they splashed through puddles in the street. None of them had umbrellas. I saw a fifth woman standing off to the side of the group. It was Charlotte Rampling. I lifted my camera and photographed her standing in the street. The group I thought she was with continued down the street without her. I photographed her again. The street was wet and shiny beneath her feet. She was more beautiful than I had ever seen her before.

She must have known all along that I was watching her because she looked up at my window and asked, "Got any dry socks?"

I opened the door and she stepped in, shivering a little as I helped her out of her dress and towel-dried her hair. She slipped into one of my old t-shirts and a pair of my jeans.

"You look extraordinary," I said.

I'd just done laundry that day, so my sock drawer was filled with fresh and still slightly warm socks. I fished through the pile for my thickest, warmest pair and handed them to Charlotte. "Mmm," she moaned after pulling them over her feet. I leaned forward and kissed her. "I like to be inside when it's raining too," I whispered in her ear.

"Would you mind waterproofing my shoes?" she asked. I took an old shirt from the pile of old shirts in the corner and looked around for the mink oil. "Here," she said, handing it to me. I sat down on the bed next to her and applied mink oil to her shoes in a circular motion. As I worked the oil in deeper, Charlotte ran her fingers through my hair and massaged my shoulders. Raindrops pelted the roof and tumbled into the gutter. I imagined the rain barrel filling up and the two of us in the morning ladling fresh rainwater into hand-blown blue goblets, drinking on the porch as the birds began to wake and the sun rise into the sky.

I put my shoes outside the door after I finished waterproofing them. The smell of the mink oil gave me a headache and I didn't want to ruin the night. I was afraid, at the time, of finding myself enclosed in tight spaces: rooms with unfamiliar exits, jobs with poisonous ruts, anything that threatened to consume me with suffocation. It wasn't the finality of death that frightened me, but the claustrophobia of dying, the possibility that I might find myself in an irretrievable situation and no other option but panic at hand.

I wanted to live a beautiful life. I looked for that which preserved the wide-open plane of possibility: rooms with familiar exits and days without obligation or fear. Charlotte offered me the blankness of eternal possibility. She was everything I had ever sought.

After a long bout of insobriety, I decided to purchase the train ticket. No, I had not been drunk, I had simply been unconscious and had closed myself off from the world of experience. My travel agent looked tired. Her eyes betrayed the fact that she had allowed herself to be penned inside a cage for too long. I found it strange that even a travel agent could find themselves boxed in.

"Bon voyage," I said to her, because she had neglected to say it to me.

Charlotte would be waiting for me at the station.

POLYESTER SPUN RED HORSE

I was in the park, taking pictures, and I offended someone. They took me to a den behind the sandboxes. I recognized The Curator immediately, but he acted as if he was seeing me for the first time. "What have we here?" he asked, and spit into the fire. There were three apprentices seated around the fire. They laughed when the question was asked. I noticed some movement in the shadows outside the orange glow of the flame. Murky figures seemed to be pacing back and forth, as if deep in meditation, as if waiting to return to an interrupted narrative. My hands were bound and I was forced to my knees.

"Pray," The Curator said. I closed my eyes and silently moved my lips to appear as if I was something more than a crafty pagan.

"Stop," he said, after some minutes had passed. "Untie him. Bring him tea." One of the guardians cut the cloth ribbons from my wrists.

To stay calm I listened to the sound of the wind blowing outside the entrance of the den. A radio was turned on, but sounded as if it was far away, or at the bottom of a very deep well. I wanted to run but knew that if I ran I would be cut down.

A guardian emerged from the shadows with a silver tray, on which were a pot, cups, and a small plate of cinnamon sticks. He set the tray down before the fire and poured two cups of tea, a green brew with a heady yellow scent. One cup for me, one for The Curator. We drank, but I didn't know whether we were drinking to a bond, a separation, a beginning, or an end.

The sound of the distant radio was replaced by the closeness of rattling dice and dropped coins. I leaned forward, took a cinnamon stick from the tray, and put it in my mouth. The Curator followed suit and did the same. I wondered: had I offended him by reaching first? If so, he did not react or say anything. I decided to find out where I stood with The Curator by asking him a question.

"May I photograph you in the light of the fire?"

He poured himself a second cup of tea from the orange clay pot and sighed a long sigh that was neither a sigh of contentment nor a sigh of defeat. I was still unable to determine my position inside the den, despite the fact that I knew I had offended someone outside.

"You have taken too much," The Curator said, and winked. Was the wink a sign or a feint of significance? I said nothing more, not wanting to press the issue too hard, and I realized, in the dice-broken silence, that I was about to nod off to sleep.

When I opened my eyes I neither knew the time nor whether I had been drugged, but I found myself swinging gently in a white net hammock strung between the sandy orange walls of a narrow cell. Three candles burned on the floor, and a cone of incense smoldered on a small red plate in the corner. The wisp of smoke that rose from the black cone was green, and when I noticed its color I was struck by a sudden awareness of time, an awareness that I did not know what time it was or how long I had been in the cell.

I realized that there could have been an endless succession of such cells, one next to the other, exactly like mine, so similar was it to the generalized notion of what a cell should be and how it should be arranged. My camera was gone. There were no windows. My shoes had been replaced with soft sandals, my shirt and pants with a white smock. Except for the hammock, there was no furniture in the cell, which seemed to me to be an odd choice for use in a holding room or prison. I could have easily hung myself in the hammock's net to avoid whatever fate was being arranged for me beyond the heavy wooden door.

I was not one to think in terms of such drastic measures, however, and I knew nothing about the potential perils that might be in store for me. I chose to remain sedate and prone in the swinging comfort of the hammock. If they wanted me, they would come for me, was sure of that. I might have lay there like that for days.

The candles and incense quickly burned out. I became hungry and delirious. I was unable to think in terms of escape, but busied my mind with distracting thoughts about restraint and preservation. I meditated and studied the landmarks inked permanently onto the map of my life: old friends, old faces. Later, when the door finally swung open, I knew that I had begun to suffer from the first hallucinations of a man who has decided that he is ready to die. The Curator stared at me from the frame of the open door. He, too, was wearing a white smock identical to my own. I thought perhaps it was the beginning of a ritual, but The Curator merely asked me a simple question instead. "What do you think you are doing?" he asked.

"If you are not going to free me," I answered, "I am waiting to die." The Curator sighed, just as he had sighed while drinking tea next to the fire.

"You have taken too much for granted," he said. "We put you in this cell because you were tired and needed rest. Your door was closed, but it was not locked. You are free to leave at any time."

My eyes traveled past The Curator's head to a point inside a swept circle of white sand, around which sat a group of men dressed in white. They all seemed to be intent on what was about to take place inside the circle. I knew then that there would be a ritual, that The Curator was lying to me, and that I was about to be sacrificed, but a hand was raised to the ceiling and the shaking dice somehow caught the light of burning candles like glowing chestnuts left too long in a fire. I asked for a glass of water and my camera. I wanted to have a picture of my ignorance. I wanted to capture the fleeting glimpse of my beginning.

Again, and for the first time.

A STICK OF WILD OLIVE WOOD

Solimbo watched from his shop as the procession passed. Their faces were caked with dust. It had been a long trek across the desert. Only a few of the camels survived. At Makeba, the water tender refused to let them drink, and when the drivers walked towards the well, he raised his rusty musket and threatened to shoot the first man who touched a drop of water to his lips. They turned and whipped the dust at the feet of the camels, tried to push them faster and harder than they should have been pushed. All but nine had died.

Solimbo imagined the trail of carcasses along the Southern Passage. "In future years," he thought, "they won't need a compass or stars to guide them. It will be easier to follow the path of bones. The desert has broken them, so there is no reason to go to the marketplace today. By the looks of it, there won't be an auction." He returned to his weaving that, unlike the sickly camels, was already paid for. "The tapestry will not die for a lack of water," he thought."

Solimbo hummed as he worked the pedals and threads. His head often nodded with fatigue, and finally he closed his eyes and fell asleep, while his fingers continued to work. The weak legs of nine camels shook beneath the weight of their shared journey's burden.

Kali let her thoughts wander as she sat in the park, where she knew she would be able to avoid Sadib's sad stares. The sound of the fountain's falling water lulled her into a calm state of mind where loss's vocabulary lost its ability to inflict pain. Her eyes traveled from statue to statue, until she was concerned only with the solidity of the stone's lines that carved out an arm, a nose, an ear...

"The softness of stone," she thought, and turned her attention to the old men who spent their days sitting on benches around the fountain, playing chess, reading day-old newspapers, lost in the thoughts of silent stares.

Kali saw a hardness in their aged faces that was absent in the sculpted stone faces. It was a look in the eyes, a sum total of loss and sadness that made these men appear to be less alive than the park's statues.

She wondered if Sadib would end up like these old men, all of whom must have one day been in the position to carve out their lives in forms pleasing to their expectations and desires. She didn't think that Sadib was capable of succumbing to the same forces that had broken the men in the park, but watching him suffer after the loss in the desert made her realize that there were winds strong enough to blast the strongest stone down to its original blank form.

Kali contented herself with the thought that Sadib would eventually come out of his silence and that he would explain to her the source of his lament. Until that hour, though, she must be patient and wait. A dog barked at an old man who reached down to pat its head. Kali walked quickly from the park, not wanting to be touched for a moment longer by the sight of vulnerability and broken lives. She walked to the market and bought the ingredients needed to prepare Sadib's favorite foods. She decided that it was time for her to do what she could to bring Sadib out of his reverie.

"The statues don't lie," she thought, and walked home with a full basket of food in each hand.

Sadib's camel had died in the middle of the trek. Nothing lifted Sadib from his dark mood as he walked behind what was left of the herd, not the sight of Selonia's waters, not the face of Solimbo's storefront, not even the promise of Kali's healing hands. Too much had been lost in the desert for the loss to be replaced so soon. The hyenas had swarmed around the fallen camels and found reason to laugh, but Sadib's gaze was etched into a remote plane of sadness. Kali brought him tea and left him to be alone with his thoughts. She knew better than to question what she read in Sadib's eyes, and returned to her room without trying to speak to Sadib. She sensed that the journey had devised its own course of sorrow for Sadib to follow. She felt it in the house's stone floors, in its high white ceilings, in the silk that hung around the beds. Sadib was beyond sadness. The desert had spared him his life and the lives of a few of the herd.

"Not enough for profit," he thought, "but enough to be thankful to have survived." He filled his pipe and breathed the smoke until his blinded sight's heaviness was lifted. Images passed across his mind, but he let them drift uncaptured until the one he knew he was waiting for arrived.

In his vision, Sadib saw himself kneeling next to a reflecting pool. When he looked into the water, he did not see his reflection, but a patch of green trees surrounding a white tent. He lifted the tent's flap and stepped inside. Kali was there, seated next to a fire, but it was not the Kali he knew. This Kali was old and withered, her face's beauty replaced by deep crags and wrinkles, and he was an old Sadib.

His bones ached and his back was so bent that he was unable to stand up straight. A pauper's meal of sheep jaw and gruel boiled in a pot above the fire. It had begun to burn. Kali's sense of smell was gone so that she was unable to smell the smoke rising from the bottom of the pot. Sadib was overcome with sadness. He leaned forward and stirred the pot.

Kali had fallen asleep on a blanket next to the fire. As Sadib spooned the sparse meal onto wooden plates, Kali gasped her final breath and died. Sadib knelt beside her, held her hand, and closed his eyes.

"Sadib," Kali said, poking him in the ribs. Sadib looked up into Kali's face, young and beautiful, and lifted his arm to invite her to lay down next to him on the mat.

He said nothing about the vision, and fell asleep with her in his arms as his mind tried to come to terms with the journey's full circle.

THE GEOGRAPHY SENDER

He had walked miles through the arid plains with only one skin of water and now, as he stood on top of the edge of a cliff looking down at the clusters of thatched huts below, he knew that he would never escape himself.

The path through the desert had not been without dangers to keep his mind on what he was doing. As he walked and tried to forget his thoughts, scorpions, snakes, and huge crab-like creatures with snapping mandibles rose from holes in flashes of magnesium white flame to distract him from the purpose of his journey.

These dangers were not great enough for him to completely forget why he had come to the desert, nor were they small enough to allow him to stop thinking all together as he had wished, and to his chagrin, he sometimes could not tell if the dangers that rose from the desert to confront him were real or if he was hallucinating them.

Someone down below came out of their hut, looked up at him and waved. He raised his hand and waved back, not sure from so high up if it was a man, woman, or child. He found a pile of stones that marked the beginning of a path down the side of the rock face that led to the village of huts below and began his descent, not sure if he should go down or turn back and head in the direction from which he had come. Every step down the side of the cliff felt as if something, some force or instinct, wanted him to turn back.

"It's just the fear," he thought, and concentrated only on his footsteps and the loose stones beneath his feet. The world shimmered and flexed around him as if it was made out of funhouse mirrors. When he looked, though, he did not see his own reflection but the reflections of all the people he had known and left behind when he set out on his journey. That life was far away now. When he was there living it, walking around in its mist of confusion, he did not feel that it had anything to do with him. Now, though, in the desert, the life he had left behind seemed to be a very tangible and life-like thing, as if only by leaving it behind could he appreciate and believe in its existence and his place in it. Voices of all the people he knew screamed out at him from every rock and grain of sand. On the horizon, when he looked up from his feet, he saw the people who were important to him, who he had taken for granted or been unable to fully fathom in their proximity to him. Now, in their mirage forms, he saw for the first time how real they were and how much he missed them.

Walking by the light of the moon, he spoke to them out loud, while on the other side of the world they went about their lives and only knew that he was gone, not where he was or what he was doing. They were beginning to grow accustomed to his absence and one day would forget him almost entirely. They would not know they had grown in stature inside of him and that they now appeared as giants standing on the horizon, and that although he knew he had no choice but to press on with his journey, he also wanted to be back in the world he was trying to escape, asleep in her arms, hours from the dawn.

"To have walked to the end of the earth and found you there," he thought, and laughed out loud. He had seen her one day and knew that, like him, she had no fear. What he did not know, though, was whether she had known fear and learned to conquer it, or if she was not afraid because she did not know what fear was. Or, like him, had she learned that fear was what led one to keep on going from day to day, and that after each new level of fear there were higher levels waiting to be experienced and conquered as well. Her eyes looked at his without looking away. He had immediately wanted to avoid her, knowing instinctively that if he fell from her cloud he would fall forever and never land on solid ground again. Now, as she stared down at him from the stars and waited for him on the horizon's sliver tightrope, he knew that he had made a mistake and that by choosing the desert instead of her, he would never exist again.

In her arms, he had wanted to overthrow everything and build a new world, but his loneliness had gone on too long and become his natural state of affairs. He wanted to look back and see her footprints following his in the sand as he trudged on towards his unknown destination. When he looked up, she was dancing on the horizon, leading him on with her hands and her eyes. He lowered his head and walked on into the night. The wake of footprints he left behind in the sand was smoothed over and erased by the desert wind. A jackal followed his scent. It was curious to see what kind of creature this was. It wanted to look this creature in the eyes and laugh at its foolishness.

He did not know that he was being followed, so he did not quicken his pace and did not look back. His goal was in front of him, though he had no words yet for what it was, place or person, that he wanted to find. A silver beetle fell from the sky and landed at his feet. It glowed like an illuminated diamond. He picked it up and swallowed it. He could feel its warm glow in his belly and when he looked up he saw himself dancing with her on the horizon.

She was whispering in his ear, telling him something important, a secret. He ran, trying to get closer to hear what she was saying, but the sun began to rise over the horizon, and as her face and his disappeared along with the stars, all he could hear was his own voice, mouthing the words, "Slow down. Wait. Slow down." He wanted to tell her that he was immortal and that he would wait for her forever.

He climbed his way slowly through the rocks on the path and down towards the village below. The jackal thought about how fear was its own poison and that a mirage is always the image of something lost that can be found again in time. It watched from above as a robed woman met him at the base of the cliff, held out her hand to him and led him to her hut, where they disappeared behind a curtain that hung in the doorway.

On the other side of the world, she was not thinking about him. She was looking out her window, thinking of nothing.

THREE: THE CAGE WRITINGS

"And it was always drainage for angels...."

Antonin Artaud, "The Execration Of The Father-Mother"

"As you have probably heard, I am no novice.
A good deal of stone passes through my hands."

Cavafy, "Sculptor Of Tyana"

"Now I have reached the Certa, a noted cafe about which I
have much left to tell."

Louis Aragon, *Nightwalker*

INTRODUCTION: THE CAGE

In the summer of 1990 I had two campus jobs at the University of Massachusetts, Amherst, where I had just finished my first year of graduate school in the M.F.A. Creative Writing Program. In the morning, from nine until noon, I was a Lab Assistant for a pair of scientists working on ways to use fish as fertilizer. For three hours every morning, I stood at a sink in front of a window with a view of a pine tree, a small patch of sky, and some buildings across the way.

I listened to the morning jazz program, cleaned test tubes and laboratory glassware, and mixed up some kind of smelly brown fluid called agar. Sometimes I worked slowly and patiently stared out the window for long periods of time while the music played and the pine tree's branches bobbed gently in the hot summer breeze. Sometimes I worked quickly in order to escape that hot and smelly room for the calm and quiet of the campus subdued by another long New England summer.

Halfway through that job, a scientist arrived from Romania to work with the scientists who employed me. He was an older man in his mid-fifties, with bushy draconian eyebrows and a thick accent that made it difficult for me to understand what he said despite the fact that his English was quite good. The week he arrived, we were told that two tons of fish had arrived for us to grind.

We donned thick rubber gloves and white smocks and went down to the basement and the huge coolers where all kinds of strange things were kept chilled or frozen, and where it was good to stand for a while before returning to the heavy humid air that hung over the valley and made the days and nights feel longer than they actually were.

We took the fish to the grinding room and proceeded to heave them into the grinder. They were big fish, three or four feet long, and they stank as if they had been left somewhere to rot for a few days before being refrigerated and sent on to us at the lab. The grindings oozed out through a spout on the side of the grinder and fell in thick goopy clumps into the bin we had positioned to catch them.

All the time we were doing this the Romanian scientist was telling me stories about the revolution in his country and how he had shot at government troops with an old World War II carbine.

At noon, I raced home on my bike for a quick lunch and a few minutes of MTV, then returned to campus at one for my afternoon job as Recreation Supervisor at Boyden Gymnasium, where I was a weight room supervisor in a fenced-in cage filled with exercise equipment.

It did not matter to me that the temperature inside the building was usually ten or twenty degrees hotter and twice as humid as it was outside. It did not matter that I was making six dollars an hour, or that I had to wear a maroon polo shirt with the Boyden Gym insignia and the words "Recreation Supervisor" printed in white ink over my heart.

All that mattered to was that I had free time to read and write, a desk and a chair, and little or no direct supervision. I used my time well that summer, reading nearly a hundred books. My daily routine in the cage was simple. From one to two or three I read, from two to three or four I wrote, and from three to four or five I lifted weights, played football, basketball, or racquetball with some of the other "Recreation Supervisors."

It was not an easy regimen. That cage often felt like a cell and contributed to plenty of existential detours of thought, and it seemed like I was always hungry, that there wasn't enough money that summer to keep a well-stocked refrigerator, but by the time the new school year had arrived I had written a hundred poems and prose pieces and both felt and noticed a visible change in the strength of my body.

I had worked myself into shape and release from the dark humidity of that cage at the end of the day allowed me to celebrate more freely than I normally would into the late hours of the hot summer nights when we'd wander the fields and back roads, drink beer in a dark sweaty club on Route 9, dance to reggae music along with the migrant tobacco workers from Jamaica, shouting each other on to push ourselves further, to forget the chores we needed to perform each day to earn a living, and to press on towards dawn, when a few hours of sleep would have to suffice before it was time to get up and return to the idle but productive calm of the laboratory sink, the jazz on the radio, and the heat of the waiting cage.

THE CONTENTS OF A TIN BOX

We are not trapped in a cage with an open door. The potential of prison and love lie not in their manifest realization but in the expansion of threat that hangs above the head, a cloud of chains, a chain of clouds. Our sitting is equipped with literature, our love is still an unfurnished room, stacked to the ceiling with sealed, unopened boxes. What is inside them? Time? Can we afford to wait for what we think we are waiting for? Thinking about you improves the sensory quality of my bleak surroundings: the gray cage, the broken chair, a desk with no drawers. I was walking in Brussels one day, spending my time wandering, hours and miles from you, looking around, exploring alleys and open doors. I heard music and found myself backstage, watching a symphony rehearse. I was able to walk unseen on a balcony above the heads of the musicians and looked down from the darkness above, where cigarette smoke lingered in its own ring-fingered haze.

A minute, an hour, a day later, I returned to the street and found that my view of the world had been altered, slightly, by the efforts of the music-makers in that dark hall. They were content to sit, to exchange glances with the conductor, to breathe life into their musical text's manuscript, while I continued to wander. We are waiting for the things that only waiting will produce. Everything is happening on different levels, unseen but happening.

Certain voices come from the distance, carried on the backs of pigeons riding red tricycles. These birds are the messengers of grief and laughter who in later days will gather at the top of adobe walls bearing glass placards that say: "This is not an entrance." or: "School is not a net of grapes." or: "Bustle never made commodity."

Some of us will walk away in mortared relief, reminded to take note of the ceiling mural, a painting of a face turned towards the sky. Its wings are spread, and blue fills the eyes with reflection.

We want to take wing and find exits into entrancement.

AND THE ZONE OF BLACK

On the threshold, about to roll open a new floor of potential carpet, the first try, the new way, an end to past searches, a fair trade for the barterer: my time and skin for yours. The area has no bounds. It is a patch of pure silk with lemon and whiskey as adornment. In this world there can be found, in certain aqueducts, ample reason to rest, subtle inspiration to sleep. We've discussed our dreams many times, the two of us, none of them amounting to much in our possible world. Our story together searches for resolution, but there are few such outlets into a loosening of the constricting form. We push, pull, enter and exit. Large circles of wind hover over the grass. Glass bottles shatter and splash against the sides of our perfect shower. The mood will pass, the stone-filled basket will be delivered. A black beetle will polish itself for the exhibition of nerves.

Will sleep erase the head's rush into spiral or make matters worse by extracting a tooth? Paths are open to those willing to become followers. In that cloud there, a reclining woman, a flock of birds floating past her thigh. Who or what do you imagine yourself to be? Allow the curious doors to flap open: the field below will surely transform itself into an event of meaning. A swan waits to hear the singing, but what swan, what singing? Ah, the bluff cool of details and unfilled blanks: *this* swan, *this* singing.

A triangle of cheese and tomatoes captures our attention in an iceless liquid of immersion. These colors are not wanting, but endless books rise into the sky while a cathedral elevator descends willingly into snow. I'm going to take a chance and open up to you now: my carpet has a following. It has sunk to the bottom of the pond. You'll find me there, clinging to its tattered edge, breathing through a long straw as I try to remember what the sky looks like at night when you roam alone and wonder where I am and why I am not easier to find. The reason is this: I am hidden beneath the surface, which you must barter with and part to receive the spell of my knowing glance.

SHE WAS RUSSIAN AND LOVED SNOW

Cold water spills from the hot machine when you are in the thoughts of others. How can you say no when your quote was meant to be yes? I love to leave the first page blank. Only books smell like that.

When I met you, the top of the glacier was frosted with mint toothpicks, each of them stuck into a red cherry, eyes filled with cinnamon tears.

The wild white Bengal tiger eats deer, buffalo, and smaller animals. I'd like to see your eyes reflected in the wings of my compass, as sad as that may seem in relation to the orange section of strings.

A lime of music is a switch of pain, ripped like bark across the knee while hope is kept in a mind hat waits to be cordoned off and kept private, safe. Sadness occupies much of the landscape.

Turn to the sun: waiting is not so much a chore as it is a trick of endurance. A thousand eyes watch. Five hundred people wait for your call. Doubt and difficult breathing disappear in the salts of Caribbean waters.

Little one, I cry for you, I am not myself without you, I am dying without dying. Such a waste, but I'm chained to your chair. It knows no repose, its boundary is silent: I may never know you or meet you.

I've been preparing to talk, to tell you everything I know. I insisted on leaving to arrive where you are. Our song entered four ears, can't you tell? Are you awake to my envy? Did I wander endlessly only to arrive no closer to your street?

You arrive from odd angles, chiseled into a stone diary, a slow week, an old couch, remembered flesh, defiance. You become a pocket of resistance behind pursed lips and squinting eyes that doubt the fallen penny.

I traverse the square for clues to your disappearance. A tree there is slowly dying. The gardener comes after midnight to bring it slowly back to life.

THIS GHOSTLY TRIANGLE
IN THE STEROPTICON

In the soul of every page is a story to be sold for sacrifice to the proper scribe, an initialed encounter with a woman of bearable solitude, a rug beaten free of its extraneous dust.

She eclipses the mundane need for gray identification and shoulders the cold water's heavy demands without gasping. Everything in her smirk is death, but the kind that brings life after the lung's initial collapse.

To stretch and flex is not the same as binding one's oath to the blood arm of conspiracy. Her promises are vague enough to insure that promise itself remains misunderstood. The challenge is to hold out for fulfillment and unbroken ducts.

A pigtail's longing for tied ribbon comes with the adjunct's defensive stance. Perversion's illuminated skin peels without flaking when two have consented to life's challenged demands. Everything is about everything else or nothing in particular.

An extra three hours of waiting rarely disturbs the chances of encounter. She sits on hills to smoke cigarettes, she walks without knowing where to go, she sighs while waiting for broth to boil, for something other than the daily routine.

She smiles because she knows a smile flies towards isolated continents with wings of its own design, because there is no better way to initiate an encounter than to forge one's own opening and turn short breaths into sighs the width of calm and fit sleep.

Panic breeds distrust. An aged notebook contains the secret that will reveal longing's exterminating elixir, but this notebook has yet to be discovered in the ruins of some crazed monk's vital day. A little at a time eventually adds up to the whole.

Tools that rust without production are signifiers of the differences shared between stories without a care for each other's sinking plots. Her hope is as reliable as a dissolving fence, a barrier between the body's rind of fortuity and its acceptance of fate's quiet departure.

At one point, the ghost arrived at her door, but she turned it away. Some of her things were found washed up on the shore: a spool of red thread, a black shoe, a small brass sundial, a lucky horse tooth suspended in honey inside an amber medicine jar.

The items were placed in a velvet bag and filed in the museum's archive while from another ocean on the other side of the world, she emerged with bare feet to test the water's pearled sand.

The one who had waited long without smiling risked the crack of a grin and welcomed his permanent guest home with a string of live flowers.

BALTHUS INVENTED BY COLOR

The mask is a difficult procession. How does it feel to be one of the veiled strangers? There were skeins being passed from hand to hand, as if the tiger had wished for its spell to work. What is one more day of an unvaried condition when the pace of rotation orbits without pausing to stop and consider? Nothing is lost from gain that isn't gained back from loss.

There was a momentary flicker of recognition between the images mingling in the wings. The body was claimed by a young woman who drove it off on a horse-drawn cart filled with straw to soak up the blood. A group of old men filed past the window. Each of them spoke a different language, except for the oldest, who walked at the end of the line whispering translations to himself. Only the nondescript stranger asked, "Why not me?" The headache will not abate and the breath is short. Sometimes a line is devastating, like when you are alone and think you are happy to be alone, and the line you read is about loneliness. Then you think: you ends with you. A carton of eggs has no choice but to be painted into the littered canvas. It is already too crowded for the minstrels to play, much less wander.

She went away with an empty feeling. It had been the richest night of her life. She didn't know that he didn't like the way she'd made it so easy to get to her. Behind the screen sat a table of daisies. He sensed that something was wrong, like a congregation of bad habits. Facing the painting closes a corridor, while facing the corridor closes the painting. Picasso in wings. Dali's trepidation. Rilke's masks. Isabelle Eberhardt's funeral. Lotus, the chain of souls.

When does the mulling end and the singing begin? You don't want to know the wrong kind of stranger. Her horse was dappled, saddled to pull its cart without envy. In death, there is also a dining room, and the double edge between this woman who knows the library's extremes and the muscle that comes undone when released of its tight cord of swallows.

SAMURAI BY SEPTEMBER

There is a tract on your windshield about the reliability of combination locks. Did you ring the bell or sleep with the fur trader? It's funny, kind of, how plants die when left untended.

I worked within sight of the tower. The church is still closed but you can watch the bells ring. For an unemployed priest it is a special treat to hear the noise of his hometown. It's also good to be lost in a book. That kind of loss is good, like dry lumber.

High above the ground sex is more precious, its infinite value undoubted by grounded claims of aversion. An hour sifting through your hair is more valuable than gold. My letters reek of your presence. That type of cloud is reassuring, a fixed clock unfrozen in winter.

Time is our train. I have more and more to say but want to say less and less as I draw up next to the end of coal. There's no reason to waste our breath speaking when we are content to stay in the library until closing time. Again I will meditate on you.

I expected to see you today at the café, but your table was empty, even of its ashtray. Steel slides smoothly inside the workings of many machines, yet we find it impossible to function so effortlessly together. I'd sweep into the room like a Grand Duchy if I thought it would do any good, but my one desire is for you to find me wearing my own unintentional garb. Our splash's echo remains unmet on gravity's shore. There are few secrets to be dug out of flowerbeds. The stray mound possesses something treasure-like.

Nothing is as it seems. Everything is like it is not. I look to you to sharpen the knife. I look to your first cut to wake me from the dismal dream of delay. We can count on the clock's hands to break eventually, but ours, which have been split from the beginning of time, must come together soon for the echo of their clapping to be heard in the harmonics of Lascaux Cave.

A KIND OF UR-TEXT

Like the love rising inside me, cooked and lost in a bag of similar golf balls, she considered my stack of books, aware of the promise behind my garb. I existed more in the future than my checkered and spotted past. "We should taste the honey," she said while I laced flowers into her dress with a pine needle. "Consider the mushroom. A brilliant example of the terms we've been discussing."

She stood and shed her plume in a cloud of acrid guitar smoke. I blinked my eyes and nodded. For two months I taught her English. She taught me French but I was a lazy student, the unhatched egg, the listing cow, the veering moth. We danced in a pasture of daisies until she said, "I hate daisies. When my father died his coffin was surrounded with daisies. I bent down to kiss him on the cheek and a bee stung my nose."

I remembered the infinity of possibility that my mind had continued to overlook. "I must learn to trust again," I said. It was a quiet day at the front but the home guard still patrolled the streets. "I am exploring a mode of existence in which I do not speak, think, or express myself in any way," she said. "Do you understand me?" It took years to write the novel I threw away in a minute.

"You are overripe for something good to happen to you," she said. "Yes," I answered. "It's been years since I've been to the coast." Downstairs all was quiet, even the pacing ceramic cat. Like the ends that never meet, hasty fellowship is rarely a solved dime of contentment. Knowing which words come next is only enough to sustain the billed moment, but the river of continuity thrives on documents of inebriated length. "Did you pay the apple tax?" she asked.

"Wait," I said. "Not just yet." I struck an ironic pose of worship beneath the tree. She laughed and told me about the man like me she had never met. "I was never able to count on the potential of your existence," she said, "but here you are."

I dipped the oars and rowed.

THE SACRED BREADBOX

There were others seated at the table with him, dressed in tuxedoes and evening gowns, but he had never seen any of them before. The main course was served. He could not help but feel disturbed when he saw that the dishes were filled with live wasps, and that the other dinner guests calmly and gingerly used small silver forks to place, one at a time, the writhing insects onto the tips of their tongues.

If he knew a sympathetic ear seated at the table, he might have leaned forward in his chair and whispered something to the effect that "wasp is a difficult and complicated dish to enjoy." He noted how intent the other guests were on their dishes, as if the eating of wasp required every gram of one's concentration to prevent them from flying away before reaching one's mouth.

He understood that the wasps must have been stunned beforehand by the chef and that whatever anesthetic he had used had only partially immobilized the insects. "What makes wasp a delicacy," he knew the chef would say if he asked, "is the fact that they move around and buzz in the dish."

He also knew that if he had asked one of the other dinner guests to explain how he should go about eating the delicacy, the silver-haired woman at the head of the table would insist that, "you absolutely must not chew them between your teeth. Place them on your tongue and let them crawl down your throat. It's simply an exquisite sensation once they begin to sting the lining of your stomach."

The other guests would tap their wine glasses with the little wasp forks and murmur "Hear Hear, Hear Hear" to the accompaniment of the sleepy wasp buzz.

That night, as he tried to sleep, the sound filled his half-dreaming head. He was able to make out the dark outlines of some of the dinner guests seated around the edge of his bed. He shook his head and rubbed his eyes, but the feeling that he was trapped somewhere halfway between the reality of dream and the reality of consciousness could not be shaken. His stomach ached and his lips, when he licked them, tasted like tin. He rose from the bed, put on his red silk robe, and peered out into the hallway.

"Catherine," he said, as if expecting her to come to him, but he didn't know anyone with that name except, perhaps, as some remnant of a half-dream.

He went back to bed and hoped the indigestion would go away before dawn, when he would rise and join the other guests for the day's hunt.

THE BROTH NEVER VARIES

I must tell you now about a most incredible little village in the mountains, where one can wander through a cemetery and meet men and women of a most divergent, strange, and beautiful nature. You will have to bribe the gatekeeper with a few coins or a steaming basket of muffins, small prices to pay for the ethereal pleasures afforded to the curious visitors of this place.

I should perhaps mention that it will do you no good to go there in the day, although from the cemetery's west summit, you will have a splendid view of the village's daily balloon regatta. It is only after dark that the apparitions can be seen, and only after midnight that they can be felt as living flesh.

My evening began with a wash and a shave in front of my room's little washbowl and mirror. I detected an unusual expression of anticipation in my eyes. The knowledge of a journey or experience to come is often enough to flush one's face with happiness.

I ate a light country supper in my inn's modest dining room, illuminated with honey-scented candles. Each dish that was served to me contained spices that suggested the infinity of possibility to my palate. Every mouthful left me convinced that I was being treated to some of the happiest hours of my life. I ordered dessert, coffee, and a heady glass of one of the local resident's homemade mead.

After two sips my face flushed with a pleasant warmth. I felt like I was floating. I had as much difficulty pronouncing the name of the mead then as I do now trying to remember it on paper. Not only are things seen and remembered special to me: in my travels I have learned that what we forget teaches us how maintain an aura of mystery around the places we have visited.

I was in a most happy mood when I left the inn for my evening constitutional. I gave the cemetery gatekeeper a basket of freshly-baked rolls from the inn's kitchen. He smiled, tipped his hat, and bid me to enter. I walked slowly at first, taking in the names and dates inscribed on the headstones and, to prolong my pleasure, averted my eyes from the first apparitions that emerged to greet me.

A black cat followed at my heels. I looked from side to side, searching for the one apparition that suited me. I soon abandoned my feigned indifference and began to take in some of the beauty that floated gauze-like through the warm night. They were silent and serene, suggestive of something beyond reach, something I would feel but never fully comprehend.

The one I felt I was there to meet appeared before my eyes and led me by the hand to the soft stone of her grave, where she welcomed me into her open arms. I awoke the next morning from a heavy sleep and ate voraciously, as if possessed by the hunger of two people.

DERIVED FROM DRIED BLOOD

I stood on top of her imaginary grave and imagined myself crying about her imaginary death. I was able to mourn, though I knew I would see her reflection later that day in the glass of the metro window. My waiter brought me a saucer of milk. When I didn't immediately lean down to lap it up with puckered lips, he said, "Sir, are you aggravated?" I continued my meal in silence.

A rat walked next to the Seine, its eyes lit by flames of tea. In her reflection's sign language, she told me about a dead mouse she found in her pocket. "I've no idea who could have put it there," she said, reciting the guest list.

My back ached like a wall of trumpets. Later, I saw a dead man in the street, not far from the ruins of the old city wall. "The bell ringer," someone said. I spent the rest of the day pacing back and forth across the museum's creaky wood floors, wondering when his belongings would be put on display. It was a terrible day. "Not allowed," a sign on the wall said. A stern guard shook his head sadly when the museum director released forty-seven chickens in a room filled with sculptures and announced that farm animals were to be allowed into the galleries free of charge.

She walked behind me, applauding the director's bold move. "I haven't seen you in weeks," I said. My sore throat felt like the coarse nudity of her unkempt couch. "What have you done with your time?" she asked. I explained my novel that worked on four different levels of meaning. She smiled and said, "All that matters is that you continue to do the work." We sat at a cafe where one of the waiters set fire to a mannequin. Smoke billowed into the sky as the gathered crowd murmured, "what sex is it, what sex is it?"

Our hotel room's window offered a view of an exhibitionist's flat across the street. We ordered candles from room service. At the track we bet on a black horse. Someone opened a can of pencil shavings. We found a program under her seat.

All the names of the cast had been cut out.

A PIGEON WROTE THIS IN BLOOD

They crowded around the body. One of them suggested that it might bring luck to carve the king's initials on one of the corpse's fingers. A messenger arrived with the mortician's official scroll a death certificate written in silver proclaiming the dead man unanimously dead. Muffled laughter dispersed evenly through the crowd. They all knew that the man had died in his bed fully dressed after a long night of savagery at the coliseum.

One man in the crowd claimed to have seen him throw the green bottle from the center of the ring that hit one of the princes in the head. Another said the man had promised to marry his sister. A third suggested that the body did not deserve to be burned or buried with the royal seal and that it would be more suitable for it to be fed to the wild boar roaming the waterless moat outside the castle.

An actor was driven in from the country to play the part of the priest. Nine young girls were hired for a brief chorus. In the middle of the ceremony, cannon fire was heard in the distance. The body was lowered into the ground as the alarm to make ready was spread from mouth to mouth. Few survived the following month's fever. Those who did suffered from a strange fit of hallucinations that affected the memory. Still, they acted as if they had won a great victory.

Straw gatherers lay down soft floors for the dance. Geese were slaughtered and skewered above burning pits. Goblets were carved from the trunk of a tree recently felled by wind. House doors were left open as domestic worries made way for soft amusements. Wicker baskets were filled with beets and thrown into the crowd during the procession's advance into the main square. Distrust and love existed side by side along with a young girl's implied virginity and an old herbalist's confirmed virility.

The voice that suggested the possibility of running interference with the town's water supply was silenced. Shackles were strung between gold daggers and slow suicide, mythological manifestations of hysteria. A lone scribe was put in charge of the monastery and told to write down everything he saw. He died one day but not before he had fulfilled his dreams of sustenance and love.

It is said that a happy ghost now occupies that former house of worship that is now a factory where bullets are made.

A PAINTED FINGERNAIL'S
DANCE OF CONCEPTION

They bled the cow to death before cutting it up into bite-sized morsels. The blood was filtered twice through charcoal screens to eliminate any impurities. Special glasses, hand-blown for the ceremony and locked away in sealed crates, were arranged in circles on a square table with a black and white chessboard design on its top. Each glass received a measured level of blood.

Plates piled high with white-powdered pastries were added to the arrangement. It was implied without being said that each participant would decide for him or herself whether to eat the pastry after drinking the blood or to eat the pastry before drinking the blood. A girl, the daughter of one of the priests, burped after swallowing her measurement of blood, sending a wave of laughter rippling through the crowd. The girl blushed, curtsied, and returned to her seat neat the back of the room.

In another part of town, a similar ceremony was being performed, with one exception. Peacocks were sacrificed instead of a cow, the blood poured into specially made ivory troughs. The local farmers walked their strongest, milkiest cows into the ceremonial den to drink the blood, which was said to be rich with good omens.

The participants of both ceremonies met and gathered in the center of town. Each member of the first ceremony was given a cow from the second ceremony as a gift and climbed on its back to ride to the shore, where a prayer was offered to the sea. The farmers returned to their work in the fields. Next year, they would participate in the first ceremony and receive a cow to ride to the ocean.

Every year in that small town it is the same. The few who venture yearly to witness the sacred rite are unable to discover a flaw in the village's ritual logic and end up looking back on their stay in that town as one of the most pleasant experiences of their journey.

BIG GLIMMERS IN THE DISTANCE

Our town is without a fountain, our children are sad. The cobbler moved across the street and became the locksmith. The locksmith moved to the country to raise cows. The farmer wanted nothing to do with shoes or towns, so the cobbler shop was left as sad and empty as our fountainless square. Last year we lost the baker. There is always someone who is unable to make the necessary adjustments.

Our poor little town suffers from indecisiveness. "To Let" signs occupy most of the prominent windows. Empty spaces remain unfilled. No second wave stands up for the fallen first. We wait and watch for a third to emerge from the wings, but what wings? Our patience turns into pleated despair. We pray for the satiation of our desperate hopes, for the day when tears of happiness cascade down our streets to cleanse our long untended gutters. One day we will reclaim our town from its malaise.

At first we will not know how to live but the skill and passion we used to feel when the rivers were filled with live fish will return. New generations will replace us; the flow of water from the mountain is steady. Our river is the source of all longing. We measure the future against partial dreams of the past. Our river is ablaze with memory.

Yesterday the library burned down. Copies of our town's favorite books often make it as far as the water wheel, where the school janitor picks them out with a net. Later he dries them out at the foundry under close supervision of the librarian, who traded places with the wine merchant. It is sad to think that so many details are always in the balance but any long sleep begins with enormous pains. Our sad children trace circles in the sand with dirty toes and rusty spoons. There is little else to do, less to eat. We spend most of our time at the train station where anonymous strangers leave volumes of poetry on vacant midnight benches.

We are a sad town. Our librarian is happier than she used to be, but the rest of us, help us, please, someone help us.

A SILK TURTLE'S CHLOROFORM WASTE

"Take what you can that's given," I said, "don't belly up to the broad-shouldered fence. These things I've told you before, this acceptance of madness, undying faith in chaos, our claim for fur and justice, both equally warm and classically composed. To be afraid to express is to be afraid of silent handcuffs."

"But I want it to be so much more than just an encounter," she said. "I'll never forget you enough to remember your bad side," I responded. In the working world, a silent sill Buddha knows no play. The inn is closed for police work. There is room for a ton of fish in the back of the truck. Now *that's* a deal worth making hay for, but I was holding out for something better.

"Back to your post," she said. "But I'm not lying for you anymore," I responded. Some people don't want to be talked to and don't even say hello. They are mannequins, free of the helpless sprinting around the gates. "I want to make love tonight," she said. "You don't have to show me your identification for that," I answered.

I tried to imagine us sitting on a bench next to a pond as swans floated by. We spoke of communal living, but I am in the market where pounds of solitude sell for a premium. "I wanted to flag you down," she said to me one day, "but your brimstone had meshed with a madman's elated gait."

"If you're not laughing at everything," I responded, "you've lost your sense of humor to eternity."

LOOKING FOR ANTI-HONEY

Something gave in the wall. They avoided a tongue in the road by forking to the right. Near a grove of olive trees, they imagined peace. A salt mine suggested prosperity. Nothing reminded them of love. It was a perfect excursion. He rose to leave but returned with a rose. She refused to say what she was thinking except to observe that the rose's thorns were very sharp, the flower was dead, and that he had either killed it himself or paid someone else to kill it for him. They sat together in the library. It was snowing outside.

They watched through a window as a boy selling newspapers sneezed and dropped a fistful of change into the snow. He pushed some of the snow away, but found none of his coins, and gave up his search after a few minutes, coughing as he tramped off through the snow. "He won't make much of an archaeologist," she observed before returning to her book.

The rabbit runs fast and is quickly too far away to catch. An anonymous band plays to an idle crowd. I've got a guinea worth showing to the guard. Surely he will release us but how will we explain our tardiness to the toll collector when we have no silver, only brass?

Maybe a new bookstore will open in town. Maybe part of the void will be patched over. There is no such thing as too much gestation. Patience breeds depth while grasping at loose ends fails to make deep the shallow edge of longing. I was not transformed, an egg, sifted mule, or barnacles of doubt scraped away from traps and paralysis. I've come to be alone but gone to find you. My mouth hides from others what is meant only for you.

As a result, I seldom speak and with only infrequent authority while driving an outlaw car.

A LITTLE GREEN APPLE
WITH A WORM FOR LOVE

The poetry of expatriation is null without distance over which to gaze and pass judgment on better days. When there is a time of looking ahead there is sure to be a premonition of distant weeks where looking back is the center of strained focus. This awareness of one's future nostalgia has no name, but its strange energy suggests a form of consciousness that is free of any association with chaos. Rather, it is part of a healing process that guarantees future progress. In the games of chance and love it is the same.

Love's rules are similar to those of time. The seeker is hoping for a future of calm from which he or she can turn their gaze to the past struggle and search. Loss of love leads to tragic forms of nostalgia and regret while the gaining of love allows one to enjoy the moment without doubting its existence. Now we have caught in the net a fish we cannot handle. Its death throes rib-tingle the shimmer out of our new umbrella. We are victims of the onion and other members of the produce section. Our seeds are not their seeds. Our ideas are not their ideas. In flashbacks there were legs worth watching planted in the ground while plans were made for a return to Africa.

The symposium was rarely symbolic, a lot of standing around in rooms shelved with uncut books. The wrappers never mended what was packaged inside but only kept things well-contained. When will you run out of the gum I gave you to chew? I loved you in the moment for the conversations that carried us, the floating bench, the guitar in place of words, connection of line to hook: story of the palm and green light moving into the proper realm of being.

A GOOD DEAL OF STONE
HAS PASSED THROUGH MY HANDS

Bottled up in a mink's skin of words, unleashed upon an unsuspecting jangled clause, we seek new salutations for the new world. Our intent, though, is not revolution but *evolution*. Someone has spray-painted this message on a wall in Brussels: *Evolution Is Revolution*. Like all centers, things there appear to be quiet and calm, but much takes place below the surface. You can see the message from the windows of the tram that run up and down Avenue Louise. City workers have made no effort to erase the message. Like much that defines it, the city's aesthetic beauty is also sunk somewhere just below the surface, so that at first glance a magnificent and ancient example of architecture may appear to be so far advanced in its state of decay that it is beyond repair. In fact, the building's structure is sound, hidden beneath its flaking mask of gray paint and chipped cement. Brussels is distinctively beautiful at night when its more obvious aesthetic flaws are masked by the shadowed play of electric light. The city extends no promise to the visitor. It *is* rich, though, with the *extension* of possibility, like the open hand that draws one close to look behind a curtain. Once it has invited the individual into its galleries of strangeness, Brussels decides whether to reward the participant with a revelation of sights and beauty or to allow him or her to pass through the theatre of possibility unscathed without capturing anything that might be molded or translated into the realm of the realized. Brussels is filled with opportunity but selects the extent to which its guests will be exposed to the sub-surface structure of events. The key to this city's beauty cannot be revealed in words. You must go there, live through days of wandering amidst the stares of strange eyes on cobblestone streets, umbrellas raised and lowered in a semaphore hint of symbolic profusion as you sort through the clues, looking for the city within the city.

DRAINAGE FOR ANGELS

His question rambled on, twisted and turned, and wove in and around itself. In his attempt to make his confusion clear, his question opened up new doors of possibility that, with his limited structural plan, had not previously found enough room to flex. In an attempt to appear to be making inroads, a council was assembled and assigned the task of sorting through the many issues that his raised detail had brought forth. An election was held to determine which member of the council would lead the inquiry. This meant a national holiday for the polls to be open, which made the nation's schoolchildren happy, at least temporarily, and broke up the monotony of their usual labors which, if they knew how to be honest with themselves and their peers, they would all agree had nothing much to do with anything that really mattered to them.

Despite initial setbacks, due mostly to doubt, confusion, and poor organization, the council began to make headway in their third month of inquiry. The question was discussed frequently in both local and national newspapers, and different districts found themselves in possession of differing views as to what might be the question's most beneficial answer. The council refused to comment on the veracity of these local claims in an attempt to remain, at least implicitly, above the pettiness of district bickering. They were no closer themselves to finality, though, and kept to their work without public statement.

One day, the man who had raised the national question and discovered a level of national celebrity that had raised his style of living so high that he no longer cared about any answer that might be revealed, died quietly in his bed and left the country in an anxious state of mourning. To this day, the answer to the question continues to remain at large. The council continues to meet and occasionally release statements to the effect of progress is being made, they are drawing near the completion of their task, and that another statement will soon follow.

ANOTHER PERSON WROTE POEMS
ALL THE TIME

"You can teach me," she said, assuming too much, too soon, that I would become more to her than I was to myself. Her distraction was promising, from a humanist's point of view, but it did nothing to promote the desired aesthetic. It took time to surrender, as if surrender was even an option, the world I had created for lack of a world, and in the real world's indifferent absence where alternative realities became the friendly norm, what was left behind was forgotten and lost. Her amazement stemmed from the fact that what was most real was, by process of elimination, most evasive, and what was most evasive had found its way into her acting career. How many people can say they were an extra in someone's small film? There was no reason to doubt her veracity.

In her house, there was a small room filled with mirrors where she sat for days at a stretch contemplating the angles of her valuable façade. Her agent called to tell her the news about who she would play next. A note of dissatisfaction rested at the tip of her tongue. She wanted to behave like a sad actress, if only for a day, but the cast had already been set and shooting would begin the next morning. "As fast as the flask is filled, it will still be empty at the end of the day," she thought, and slipped into a shimmering dress made of the finest skins of pearls. The limousine that arrived to take her to the set contained its own chain of extravagances.

"A mind that drills itself full of new holes is bound to expand into its own rule of thumb," she thought. "The mystified hands that grasp at the newcomer with angry misunderstanding attempt to level her new height instead of striving to attain a calm certainty of what they touch. Things initially out of place always find a way to fit in. Sometimes it just takes enough time for the dust of a new explosion to settle." An accident up ahead, her thoughts were the only vehicles moving forward.

AN EXPRESSION OF ACTIVATED SLUDGE

Rarely are there more than two ways to slay the gray horse that has found an exit from the dangling maze. The thrown rider can walk slowly along the path. He can notice the regularity of distances between hoof prints in the sand. Every few feet a spot of blood tells a brief riddle about the horse's flesh wounds but the spot is only a drop, not enough to bring a determined steed down to its knees.

Finally the tracks will lead to a cliff's edge. The rider will sigh and peer past the abyss's smirking lip. His thoughts will focus on his loss, preventing his mind from penetrating the fog that covers the bottom of the deep valley below. He turns and follows his own tracks back to the stable where he buries his face in a mound of dry hay and sobs until the gold strands are soaked and wilted in defeat.

Beneath the fog at the base of the cliff the horse finds traces of the beginning of its refuge. A cold clear stream runs through the valley's secret village where horses are treated like kings because of their rarity. Without roads or paths into and out of the valleys the only horses to appear are those that make the leap from above. The villagers are patient. It is understood that one or two horses will appear each year so there is no need for want or despair.

What privileged hands have run their fingers the through this horse's metal hair? A thousand lines of royalty find ways to flesh out skin and divinity but there are few triptychs to describe the beheadings. A soft rain will penetrate the hardest cloud and jewels will buy baskets of gold leaf to furnish inns with burnished ceilings.

Still, and still after that, the village resonated with its own echoed calm as forks were lifted to satisfied mouths and rare moths ride without fear on the backs of these mounts. One way to slay the gray horse is to erase the words used to describe it.

A second is to forget that such words ever existed and that only now has the horse discovered the rhythm of its natural stride.

A MINUTE ORANGE FARM IN BLIDAH

I drank a bottle of bottled river water to convince myself that I was not about to be hung. The noose around my neck turned out to be a string of my wife's pearls. I sighed a sigh of relief and dropped some of them into my jeweler's open hands as a tip for his years of service. He thanked me and his wife wove a hair net for my wife to wear while enjoying the fruit of her pearls, her disjointed pearls.

I threw away the bottle and listened to my banker's boring fish story. "It was so cold in the water," he said, "the fish jumped into our boat to stay warm. Now leave me alone, I have work to do and the constable said there is a terror in Ontario."

"Excuse me," I said, "my wife is waiting for me with the oven on and I have forgotten to buy the cake pan she desires."

"If you must," said the constable. "Carry on. By the way, are you going to the lynching tomorrow? It will be great fun, some adulterers are going to dance the taut-drawn tango." He nudged me with his elbow.

"I'll think about it," I said, and made my way to the store, where I watched with a certain amount of distress as my wife held a gun to the clerk's head on the display window's close circuit television.

"Put the money in the bag," she ordered him. "All the gumballs and hairpins too."

When the police arrived I acted as if I didn't know who she was.

The constable winked and said, "It's a damn shame. She was the town calligrapher and a great baker to boot."

I tried not to flinch or tremble and ran home to wait for her one allowed phone call.

"Honey," she said when the phone rang. "I'm in trouble. Turn the oven off and take the kids to Grandma's farm. Tell Toby the worst has happened. He'll know what to do. That should give you time to get back here before morning."

I wept a bit and did all she had told me to do and drove back to town just in time to see the rope go taut.

"My wife," I thought. "My poor wife. You never got to wear your string of pearls."

I walked home a sad and lonely man and opened my mail and a bottle of bottled river water and closed my eyes. The doorbell rang. It was my wife.

"No, silly," she said, "they hung an adulteress. I'm just a common household stick-up artist."

She planted a kiss on my neck that made me shiver so hard with my spine's love for life that the pearls fell from their string and rolled across the hardwood floor towards the brown paper bag with the cake pans inside.

BLACK ROT IN CRUCIFERS

"To hope and never have is a revolving door of sour spice." The executioner's first and last line of poetry before he was put to the stump by an able apprentice...

The head fell into a green basket and was quickly delivered to the caves for preservation. The basket weaver who had been commissioned for the occasion smiled proudly to himself. His wicker had rattled properly without tilting or dumping the head's heavy load when it fell.

His task was complete and when the execution was over he rode slowly out of town on the back of an old donkey just as a robed monk walked through the gates late for the execution where he was supposed to say a few sacred words over the body.

The monk breathed heavily and mumbled angry words to himself when he saw by the vacant square littered with refuse that the event had already taken place and he quickly decided to find the mayor and ask to be taken to the head.

The mayor was half-asleep with his slippered feet propped up in front of the morning fire his wife had prepared for him. He was smiling and enjoying the aroma of freshly brewed coffee as it wafted through the low-ceilinged house.

The mayor had just congratulated himself on the administration of the successful and entertaining execution and was just about to fall asleep when there was a knock at the door. He rose to answer the knock himself as his wife had gone into town to enjoy a spot of brunch with some of her friends.

He was surprised when he saw the red-faced monk standing there with steam from his sweating body rising through the cold air, and was even more taken aback when the monk demanded to be taken to the cave to view the executioner's head. "Such a bother when things went so well," the mayor thought sadly as he pulled his coat over his shoulders and looked longingly at his leather chair in front of the fire. "But even a dead bear's hide sometimes requires trimming, I guess."

The mayor's wife looked up from the piping hot spoonful of soup she was blowing on and saw through the restaurant's glazed panes of glass the great-coated figure of her husband pass with the figure of a robed monk in tow.

She wondered for a moment where he was off to, then, satisfied in her thoughts that he was probably taking care of some official business, returned her attention to the spoonful of soup which, in her moment of distraction had cooled sufficiently for her tongue to accept happily.

The mayor bid good morning to the monk at the mouth of the caves and excused himself for not accompanying him further due to a certain shortness of breath and dizziness that always struck him when exposed to dark cold close laces. The monk bowed and disappeared into the mouth of the cave. He asked the keeper to be shown the executioner's head and was led to a row of numbered baskets--some of them green, some of them red, and some of them yellow. The keeper pointed to the last basket in the row and returned to his post.

The monk whispered a few words over the basket, basket forty-seven, lifted its lid and stared into the still open eyes of the executioner in which a faint glimmer of satisfaction could be seen. Although the monk didn't know it and was unable to fathom what might have led the executioner to die with such a satisfied stare on his face he reasoned that the man must have felt a trace of pride in his apprentice s skills as the axe fell.

The monk closed the executioner's eyes with the tip of his forefinger replaced the lid and turned to leave the cave. He would never know that the executioner's last thought was that his very first attempted line of poetry was not so bad and that

MALLARME/RIMBAUD

I am Rimbaud. I am Mallarme. My stomach is filled with grapefruit juice. I am walking across a field of dung. Each step brings me closer to the hole filled with rusty tin cans. Each step brings me closer to my death. The hole is round.

As a child, I stole bottles of beer and hard cider from the milk trucks, then running guns, drugs, and libations for government Mafioso. I sold them to our abbot—body of Christ, body of Christ—can't wash down the body of Christ without blood and wine...

A profound religious hallucination forced me to become a poet. I bought a used black suit, dyed my hair blue, and allowed my teeth to yellow. I pretended not to know people I knew. I pretended to know people I didn't. One May morning I bought a gun—the poetic staging of the suicide. I bought opium and for moments forgot the cold hard edge of reality.

Nerves steeled for asphyxiation, days began without me. The streets were filled with wanderers. I hired a tutor. She taught me inebriation, forgetfulness, the beauty of the moment. People I'd never seen before began to recognize me. I was no longer a ghost. I was alive. I took my gun to the forest. I was Rimbaud. I was Mallarme. Seducer of reality, embracer of possibility.

The soul of a dingo bars Babe Ruth's baseball bat from entering heaven. I slap myself on the face with a yellow rubber glove. Baking soda, my teeth's new white glimmer. Ducks in the Hudson, swans in Back Bay. Metros in every city but those under siege. The first section of the tunnel is complete. Now we must build something in it. We are transient. We are aglow with froth. We wrongly accuse our personal chaos of guilt. Mallarme is not innocent. Rimbaud is not guilty.

A dream of a ferry boat in a lingering fog, a river, then lost at sea. Rimbaud's amputated leg is not a souvenir of Modernism. Mallarme never used some of the spices found in Rimbaud's traveled lands. Rimbaud shivered in delirious fever. In winter, Mallarme dreamed, warm and content beneath heavy down quilts. Rimbaud's dream of marrying, of having children, could not be arranged.

My gums bleed. Warm milk helps me sleep. I will never be a diplomat, or I *will* be a diplomat. I can never choose the way, or I *always* choose the way. Two roads, two rivers, following their turns on a map, following in footsteps, choosing new paths. Grand sublimation, secretions of the muse. You follow it or you lose it.

I am Rimbaud. I am Mallarme. Who are you?

FOUR: THE ORANGE

The Earth is blue like an orange.
                    --*Paul Eluard*

In fullest June
a woman entered my life,
no, it was an orange.
                    --*Pablo Neruda*

Why do I live exiled
from the shine of oranges?
                    --*Pablo Neruda*

As in the sponge there is in the orange an aspiration to regain face after undergoing the ordeal of expression. But where the sponge always succeeds, the orange never: for its cells have burst, its tissues have torn apart. Whereas the peel alone flabbily regains its shape thanks to its elasticity, an amber liquid has spread, accompanied certainly by sweet coolness and scent—but often too by the bitter awareness of a premature expulsion of pips.   --*Francis Ponge*

1.

Death of our love that never was, a dwarf's breath next to the leaking fire hydrant.

A half moon is painted into the sky, but cloudy pale adders encompass its aurora to snuff out the gaze.

The black beetle feasts on a piece of stale white bread while drunk poets wobble beneath curious streetlights.

In the end, only gravestones will say you were here. The ground makes your acquaintance, then allows you to sleep.

All that is yours is within your grasp if you but act and make real your imagined plans for action.

Precision is required. You are not alive if you choose to sit on a cold stone bench when warmer perches call your name.

Take flight, ascend, move towards your end without tears of sadness. She waits for you just as you wait for her, two visions next to a broken stream.

Her dress is real and coaxes you together. Turn away from the tempting shadows of isolation.

2.

Loneliness is a hungry skunk at midnight gnawing at the trunk of a long dead tree. Patience is required to meet the woman who reads alone in the park.

Those knowing glances are confident in their footing. She is waiting for the exception to the rule.

Infinite patience for infinite kisses. Themes are not pears ripe for picking, they are reflectors of the seeker's gaze.

Each of us finds what we want to find in the acorns rolling around under foot. Someday we will look across the room and say what we mean with only our eyes.

There was nothing in the newspaper about your revelation, but every day you become more real.

I saw the look in your eyes when I held the door for you. So much anguish for promises of pleasure and connection.

Everything must go from here to somewhere else, from here to where it belongs. Silence is the only measured line.

I saw a guitarist in the scene of benches. She was hitchhiking in the opposite direction. I decided not to love her too much.

3.

What do you do in those moments when you think it's all for nothing? Tonight I met the voice of hope.

We sat beneath a shade tree in the church's quiet courtyard and listened to the traffic pass. The moon was orange.

Sometimes you feel like it's slipping away. You hold hands as you cross the street, but it isn't enough, there's an empty bus waiting on the other side.

I want to be *inside* the orange, surrounded by it, its skin pressed tight against mine. A fly rests on the sleeve of a leaf while two moths wait out the rain.

We are aware of each other. It's funny and sad the way things go. "Nothing is real," she said. All around are sisters, but their shock has worn off.

My clothes no longer make sense to me. I have grown uncomfortable in this disguise. We'll see where we are when we get out of here.

The ice road will remain until it melts in the spring. I'm going to build a fire on the other side of the mountain.

4.

I come from distant lands to claim my birthright. I approach the throne with one thing in mind: the overthrow of lethargy.

Don't give anything away. Be the idea, the grind of coal and chalk, sublime defection to the source of longing.

I want to know what you know. Mix blood. Traipse about in snow. Be silent together. Share our madness.

Too many times in the past you became their lie, relished the thought and frog-leaped into false rapture and the yellow stripe of the enemy.

The frogs that guard the pond are evergreen, rust, and hay. Blue dragonflies, the ebb and flow of the day, a stream beneath the bridge—relief and undisturbed rest.

The frog attempts to nab a dragonfly. She is wingless, lost in thought on bus 48, an open book in hand.

5.

The way flies take off from the sidewalk into sunlight, picking fresh berries from the brush, a black feather found in green grass.

Trimming a hedge, water running in the sewer grate, the shadow of a red and white fire hydrant, numbers given as names to houses; the unexpected but welcome guest.

The orange brings me back to myself. It lets my mind wander and sit perched on the window sill.

Even the frogs are calm. A little scene from life: two dragonflies sharing a leaf. Clouds pass overhead to wherever clouds go.

In this moment I know I exist. The dwarf's hands, an unwound clock three minutes behind the moment.

There were days like this in Paris, eating breakfast before the hike, falling back on tender feet, remembering the cemetery's alabaster leaves. Where is the moon?

Minutes pass away in a mass extermination. With some people I am the most me. With others, I am them.

It can be a sin, this mingling of minds, but you should never be afraid of *potential* torture.

6.

The little stone hits the big stone and bounces off. The big stone doesn't move. Illumination is a pretty word. *Illumination.*

I want to look behind the blue of your eyes. Which *me* is mine to keep? It will all pass into silence, but this is not a tragic thought. I'll go there, eventually, to find that rare gem.

You don't want shade to disrupt your light. Remember the vestal virgins, the wingless doves. The port city is tarnished in gold.

When I fall, I want to fall forever until I am flying. Can I separate myself from everything to find what is truly mine?

I had the impression that when the time came to act out my destiny, I would know how to embrace it.

An orb of light once floated into my room through acid-tainted windows. Don't suffer your love alone, it said. To the dark side of cardboard I add your name.

Something turned in the day and changed the heavy pace of misery. The sky is blue, the trees are green after a long winter.

The gasworks are aflame with flowers and horse's breath.

7.

Brutus, of course it matters. The mushroom knows my name. I quickly learned the rules. A moth flew out of the telephone's mouth.

Pearls with which to stain the eyes, sandbags to relieve the front, a sagging mausoleum lacks conviction, but a bee sting is the spreading of color.

You find yourself becoming the person you always wanted to be. In casks, they found slippers. In barrels, they found doves and opals the shape of wine bottles.

You must die to live and live before you die. Enter the orange's core. Life goes on until it is something else.

She threw the orange, but when it seemed ripe to settle in my grasp it roared past my ear on laughter wings.

When the orange's juice began to bleed across the cement edge of a stair, I knew I must drink it to live.

Although it was not the last day of summer it felt like the first full day of fall. The orange grew inside me and took my shape.

I looked across the bed, half expecting to see her shoulder, but only time slept there, waiting for me to join its monotonous embrace.

8.

I paced the room for hours until my mind could wander to sleep. She was a true enigma, the blue veil, something new from the old.

The world is made of triangles. I was awakened by the sound of grapes striking the blue aluminum awning.

I heard water where before there was secrecy. It's hard to get to the ones worth knowing, but eventually you find them, something present that wasn't before. For this we live.

On the lawn in front of the madhouse, this painful process of unknowing you. Somewhere far away, the night is happening.

Nothing remains written for long. Unwritten, *forever*. The orange eggs you on. Lethargy is for the others. Attack your plan with force and vigor.

It's time for you to decide what you are going to do, *today*. Go for a walk. Look for trouble. The masked line reveals itself in turns.

Lit from above, the plan is to escape. From below, it looks like something else, in glass, in formaldehyde.

So quickly after we met there was nothing between us. We moved too easily from the mysterious phase.

With everything revealed there was nothing left to eat. We wanted an umbrella filled with light, not passing thoughts and dark rain.

We wanted to relish each other with sincerity and conviction. Sometimes a song comes on the radio and you become the song. Sometimes you smile too late or not at all.

Do I want to be at your deathbed or you at mine? Ah, the grand contradictions! An orange autumn moon hung between two willows.

I pulled a stone from the sole of my shoe. The dogs were playing, they barked and bit at my ears.

Cows fell from the sky and landed with dull thumps. All over town, wisps of smoke rose to mark the pages of unturned books.

I saw the same girl every day standing at the corner. In my mind she never finished crossing the street.

A field of tar covered with clean white rags. The smell of a bakery. The sad eyes of a doe.

To always be on the verge of something, never knowing what it is, if you will find it, or how long it will stay.

10.

The orange peeks out without revealing its true intent, a master of disguise and contradiction.

Nude women lounge on towels in a field of blue flowers, a red sun's reflection on the face of a white moon: this is what you can see through the orange's skin.

There is a book etched into the orange's rind. It is written in a strange but familiar tongue.

Beautiful in its strangeness, it is the form of the form. Exercise the form. Go inside the box. Become the box.

Something else is there, grinning through it all. It gets better and it gets worse. What can you do with the forms you are given?

Something is coming to take you away. You're not ready to go but your bags are packed. The fruit of the orange is heavier than its skin, but the skin is stronger.

Don't you love being involved in the great big mess of your life? It's midnight. The moon's miniature is reflected on the pond.

So many secrets, it whispers, so many layers of fog.

11.

Terribly sad and terribly broken, their wheels rounded out by rusty spokes, carts filled with terrified lunatics pawed their way forward.

What is more important, what has happened or what will happen next? To regret the things you said, to not know what to say next, to be far removed from the scene.

To be welcomed into the fold, drawing no conclusions, being discreet, waiting for answers, curious to know more.

Never fully understanding, never being able to say for sure. Alone with your recognitions, not sure what to do next.

Trying something new, finding it exactly as you imagined. Skittering past well-trod paths, always questioning, never wanting to be the broken tower withered by wind.

Trying to resist the insistence of ancient languages, you describe pearls on strips of dirty paper. It all falls, in the end, into the void, undone.

Never knowing how much is left, or how much will be taken away, you wait for clarity to decide what to do next with the pair of green dice resting in your aging hand.

12.

All faces are her face, all voices her voice. Alone in her library, everything is understood.

Behind parlor walls, divine emergence, roaming vagrant angels. Tension swells. We are always beginning and ending, never knowing if we are in the middle or at the end.

You've got to face the orange, you've got to taste what's inside. Bruises are the skin's most important feature. Where the body has died, the skin must be rejuvenated.

The orange's flesh is sweet and ripe like something that has waited to happen for a very long time.

No one is spared from revolution. Even the dead reach out to remind us that behind the orange's skin is a skeleton with only a fragile center for a heart.

Oranges filled with seeds, oranges filled with creation. We row our boat against the stream past a tree hung from the wooden bridge.

Your eyes in candle flame, peering through shadow. Seeing someone you want to know, not so alone anymore. Hopeful ice turns to snow.

13.

One day the old self sleeps complacently at the orange's core. Our message is never clear and never the same.

There is much to offer in well-lit galleries, but there is also blindness, the lonely woman, the dying soldier, the moment just before the first kiss, the memory of the long lost last.

Do you see yourself on the horizon? I hear the raven's cry. You are always leaving when I am arriving, always in the center of the corner of my eye.

I want to believe in the moment, swallow the orange's seed. Someday today will be ancient history.

Everything must be rebuilt and destroyed.

FIVE: WERTHER'S 47

BOOK ONE: CLEVE'S PIKE

As appetizers, cold slices of marinated mushrooms; then mushroom soup, sometimes with piroshki made of rye flour with mushroom fillings, and finally the main course, boiled mushrooms.

--Lili Brik, 1920

CARSON'S CAVE

You're my red sky, my orphanage long ago, my suckle, my ending heart. Your endlessness comes to me by rowstrokes and pinpokes. I take tin to the dump. Geese flock to consume me.

Thirsty dogs yored of sense, bat-yawed cuttings trimmed until bereft of clogs: "Didn't care to contain Skelton's Hedge," at first The Geezer was complaining, then he sensed his unchained wilting, not to heat, but torn aheart.

Fastly ablunder she sailed across, spanking the mother, cursing the purse. Of course no relic saved such ends of twine to be halved for hanging. Mere's rose did the stinging: what little wounds there was came from flowers...from flowers.

Termitic, the lance thrown aloft: Mickle Mill set about to plunder. Jock tore out his own lobe. "What the misery, why?" The Geezer croaked. "Another future old cloak left the ashes behind?" "Yes, Padre," said I. "She took an empty urn."

UP AT NAG'S HEAD, STEAMING

We broke up the piketurn with a wrench, whinnying past the grave, twisting to scream across clover floss. Of course we weren't supposed to ride past Nag's Head without something to give: whistling, tapping cans, sanding bones. "Else the scrub was buckshot!" Teb said.

Gram was practically spread facewards, her brewed arms waving wristlets jangling their cause: "Silver Lode, The Silver Lode!" (Back in Teb's day when aces meant spades in the ground, dirt on the bones, and now her riches giving us away).

In hand what came to be carried, on her neck the little ouch can where she kept her teethies, she stopped to light a match for a cigarette. "No, come across the fern, Granny!" But not to waggle our way, she'd unplugged her castbroad ear and didn't hear. (Last year Finnegan planted mines in his soil).

Tens and nickel bits of Gram fell flush from the blast: each blood eye that fell to the ground were teethies grinning from the mulch. "Now there's a gulch where Grammy went up, and each such of us felt up to it spoked a tooth on a string from Grammy's kit."

A TILTED SKITCH, COME COURTING

Cantabee was slaking an ivory thirst when what was a bend but a bottle's end? No, not to be had by a cod and a went, she weren't waiting on old married Swurtz for long before he mentioned the old croaker wasn't enough far gone to give her a Bye Bye.

That old grouch, wended for capital, had marbles of cat gulch in her gut, but clamped down sudden in peaceway's grass instead of winging away on angel's weavers. Held nothing down but didn't nothing up either. The hag befuddled even Old Doc who'd come to say: "She'll be dead before the day."

Cantabee cuddled close to her parakeet, prayed the old crow to quick flight for sowing so soon Swurtz's quickseed. "A plight's a merry wherewent," Parson Weathers mumbled. He'd carriaged sixteen days just in time to see Jewel's sister croak beneath the plough.

Doc said: "She's done inside explodin' with blood. The old one finally made a night to dream tallow wax into. Not far from ever or after, but lest all be all, all's been ending. A day late, Parson, a day late." To make Cantabee loneliest and lowly of all: Swurtz too croaked while digging the grave.

SWAMP (DAY'S SAIL TO SEA)

Pondwise to ermine gloss, past Malaran's urbane moss, the swampthings, trees, vines, muck and such stuck to boots and buckles. Hatched eggs torn past will soon say West, he's able when he's able to paddle his own boat. Up down, the river flows, voiding the thick damp, sticking it further along.

Old man in the river runs to unicorn horns, voices thankel for the boon, and sails were set towards the sandbar's escaping berth. No wise critter comes aping his sole cluster without severing himself from his knowing, his ingrown distrust, his old blixen fear. Ease, he's got to ease her into the universe.

Your life is dripping from your vein, winding round the final turn towards the big untied Not-Not: unknotted twigsnap, at first to be bloomed and kited into dirt, later to be placed, some of us, at a better elsewhere. Sin or no sin you're backing into where you're from: the big Now-Now will walk you away and away you will stay, forever.

Mud thucked against his thumpboots. Skeeters nattered for toeholds on his whiskers. He scritched, his gestures more convinced of Hell, less to the Marycabin he thought he was sloppin' for. Somewhere's a thought in his direction, never, that is, to arrive eyewise in his ears where it's mighty long overdue and, like dough, needed.

MANCHIMP (CORPUSCLE TO CORPUSCLE)

He vented her oscillator on the third day, his fast's hungered hallucinations taking shape along with every notion he ever had: bootblacked strategems sparkling through ginrust glue, stuck fly-like to inspiral tape and humid ideas. Carefully The Old Neezer snuk around the hole hoping to dig his finger and sniff out a patent.

Curses, the bloody corpse didn't sink when it sank, it came into the bay like a surrender flag, and The Neezer rode him in like a bobbing dolphin. Townfolk recognized the bloated old Parson's face. It was his bible washed ashore days later that made them stick to the mark and give The Neezer his reward money for putting his effort out.

Fifth day of the old blow he fixed her motor. "Shoulda had her running for the whales," he told the Parson's one sane daughter midst a sturdy rain. She'd have followed the humpbacks home had he gimmied her an elbow jolt to start the ideas flirting with her jackblack, but religion had taken hold of her better sentiments without tagging the bottle along.

"Millet, millet and corn gruel!" he shouted, ounces of table salt spilling into his wounds. The rum room he'd docked to had a bay window where he saw her closing in upon his feelers. No way out for a Neezer, though, no way in for a fogged jackblack. He filled a hollow grave with unrepentant shavings, his life skimmed off the top like cream with a razor blade.

146

GRAM'S EASTER FLUME RIDE

Too busy dying to have piety grip her life, we drove Gram one day for the flume ride, Cleve's Pike County Fair. It was Easter Sunday; she'd been baking pies all her days, not for prizes, but for the buck of joy eating gave her kin. We piled the picknicking things into the truckback, young Werther squeezed between watermelon and Uncle Yack.

Cod cakes and clam bakes later, Gram spit from her tree onto a bald guffy's pate. He, looking up, seen nothing but jaybirds winking in the know, Gram their friend hid hind a hired branch.

"Kimmin' down, Ma!" Werther's Dad yelled. "Vodka's soaked inter the rind, kimmin' swaller, kimmin' swaller!" Even young Werther ate a big smile of melon. A singed crow come too close to the barbecue fire followed Gram to the head of the flume line's face: she lifted the birdy and coddled it into her purse, turned and leapt with a hooked stick onto the first free log.

Summer snow fell as Gram rounded the bend, smiling and waving. Dad sighed. Uncle Yack said: "Enough, enough." Werther dropped his cotton candy and jumped alog to follow. He rode his logsteed straddled horsewise, paddling til next to Gram in the rapids, logsurf standing.

"Yer a finky feller," Gram cawed. "Ready to ride?" Werther winked and nodded. Gram dropped her stick and flopped astride her log, raring to fly the furious rapids. They whooped, the two, and people standing by who pulled Werther out said they saw Gram go over the falls, and fly.

BAT-YAW, STITCH

"Why ain't I the lucky fellow to herd the gurdy towards the maw? Makes the waiting longer, keeps your mental hollow, your flask unlipped, lighter. Every brother should have a sister, every bell a church!" Werther bellowed. "Can't be knocking the yod for milk when the cow's plussed away."

Sun was setting, crows cawing, hunger bellying—everything was uncaring. Ergot, masks unfolded her glow: there were surprises under there, refusing the bodice's retinal tic. Spatuling the ham bones sieved through newt's lips, yawning and leaning sideways into the melt, Werther was coming up close to Drood's Mark.

"Now, there's wit in that, to be said, to be given away," he cried out, "but speculary is not the day. Nor never did the moon pitch across Molly's summer Jumping Jack."

"All of a sudden when it's all an ending, what's to make of the lice, the scritters scrawlin' to be scratched when an egg's worth a man's hand and them's laughing what can't cry?"

CLEVE'S PIKE

What was tarmacked to the warthog was enough split apart to brave the axe before coming to Beattalade's side row. There's enough to be abranch of along the sorry song's rack, and analog's dialogue's a crumbly sack, swallowing the tongue like that, alone.

Split far enough for parts to want to be, parts to want to be, not bad, but not enough of the razing, not high enough to reach for, and all and all and on, she keeps coming, she does well, and bades us pray for upside down misery.

Her eyes upon us cleave to us to decide. Hurts for hurts sake, but no Mary: stars fall around a neck, skinnying to be the rat caw. Oh, here's the lark, fixings and all, come upon the self's lifeboat—float about the glade and that glade's ruined.

Not to be outdone, the harbor master's boat clogged its chugburn through the canal. Nay, we weren't combined by the lark to be forsaking its many gleams; we're fixing to be blixened, where and when she may. Of course, no wheeling can ease hurting the way a wound sinks and inters pleasure.

TANGIBLE BILLET, -ERINE

Scrapped, but how, the Now-Now shook and Torbor's Notch swayed against the murk. Can't be halving her leaves to coin, never is the blend a victor's defeated stain. What was Cane's now belongs to a chain, cat shawl to cat shawl, noise to rake took, Betismo's fallow grain its mirrored palm.

Orange, orange, the bleating axe, butted against the forward shaft—muffled tale, muffled tale, one voice and a wording cake of soup to spine; spice. (Or is Maddigan's Curse upon the ended trace?) Run aground, telled and sinking back, this to waft: scared to be alive, scared to be dead.

Black tungsten stitched to swear night's end, not hewn, not blanket down, but buttered bread and an ending crissed across the tailor's cross. Werther's upon his gasp's regalic match. Werther's spurned by Tull's carp's pitch. Nix, but a bee'd come unplained, its sting unbloodstained. She'd stung him good, chained his jackblack to a sure Unwinding.

Glued, the new tongue's moon habits a shadow. Once there, curse not a body else the whisper blow, pure word sand, fate cape to maw smoke. Werther murked for slipshot bait, his end yoked to Sandville's ulterior motives, croaked. Silver tow and shadow row, course by course go so that a graveyard's welcome becomes a withdrawn judge.

TRIB TO A BIG PINK PIG
(UNWRAPPED, WHAT)

Hay turd, the lastic oinker, shammer of mud and lug huts. Course the critter's a lubber, no udder would drink its milk. Squirm and bones, squirm and bones: we're patting rumps for future bacon—the pigsleeves offer joy links.

As far as we could see, the oinker's brutality: in the mud it squammers, strains to be heard. Trough bent to tipping ends in noselipping: not satisfying, that, no, that note won't do. We were splashed with its jellied urn, exploded in the muck, Griddle Cake's littlest firstborn, that is.

All along we sat fencewise. No sign of a troubled birth, the piglets came plopping out in mudears, the oinker stammering beautifully her deft art: sucking piglets in an arc, laid out in her offal, sleepy piglickensin the boot—all amongst the sty a newborn family.

No names to the younglets, they'll scramble to be pigs, end averse end to haul their booties far enough to call themselves oinkers. All along the farmer expected better-- (first prize at the fair, first prize at the fair!) but all he got was a cluttered pen.

DUST

The mind's right about opening to scare the scurvy out--cusses to be worded about, melodies to save time with not a moment to behold and scarce less to be handing round about the square table.

Mems words were a played out old thought in the bottle, scared of the newt, dogged wet behind the tallow tale. Krebs filled with drinikens, snuffing down the lawn.

At first sight the melody played out the graveyard's way, then about the dog in the moon or the hand in the glove. Been playing scratched records too long to know the song, and blixens fetching to rent the yard to a gaggle.

Eyes watered hungry tears, shirtsleeves melted into stone, wrists yearned to draw blood, but the tub, the dirty tub's leaking and won't hold nothing, not water, not sand, not a hand cutting to be felled free, slit.

BOOK TWO: WERTHER & AT

Every man needs
A song with no
translation.

--Roberto Juarroz

BACK TUBWATER BACK (CREATION TALE)

Candles dipped from swollen river gum, tar, and clay: now there's a dinosaur mix, come to poke fun into extinction, the sad way, spacerock pounded into dust and indistinction, gone forever Bye-Bye.

A biggest Then-Then crosschecked us then, with barely a possibility to fly, much less wander around in the brine. Yes, it's a long way to go yet until Werthers and Blixens fetch to screaching screamly Come-Comes and Now-Nows. (We won't mention the sunstroked clouds.)

Passage next into a country of canyons, little flecks of Yon-Yon, kin to mincers and sucker fish, bottom fed past time changes and the newt's way of surfing up to hello the sun, running into the realm of psalmless days instead. Were that the why for us all, we'd be lesser things than we are, not even in the KnowDrink.

Of course it didn't work that way. Here She is, there He goes: Blixens sainting to be Werther'd, Werthers waiting to be Blixened, scritching from a stone cathedral's musty vault, skittering into warm alms and ahs, sighbodies against the grain of NotNight, loving and now-knocking, rounding pull fish to pull fish, lip to lip…making odds and eggs.

KNEELING BUS (IN THE DRINK)

Five for six, you just got to say no to some yeses. Wandering down the road, eyes meeting eyes, some lead to nothing, some to the Big Knowing. Knowing can't be undone from its jar-web: the jackblack never forgets where it's been, it comes upon its chalky stumps in the midst of good times and bad, low or no tide.

Then came the broken bough. He always thought he could fix it, but broken never mended well without staining blood and eyes with lead. He couldn't nix that wound without chasing his racing sanity. Then another option came groveling at his feet: beneath a gray sky lazy with damp he rubbed his nose into grass and smelled the dirt.

Rows of pine trees toothpicked at field's edge and there, where gray mated with green, winter wind shooshed to spoil the first days of spring. Startled by a shotgun bird-caw he plexed his eyes upon the old church tower on the hill and white-washed rugby posts pointing to the sky.

Wing-flap and wind-shiver remembered him back to life. Too cold then to enjoy the sparsity of No-Thought, he coughed and thought of food and began walking again, into town past little shop windows where sated eyes stared out from inner warmth.

That month then was the last of winter's noose before spring presented herself like a beadstring round his neck, aglow.

GRINDING TO A HALT
(IT'S THE HUMIDITY...)

At had bit the cud of Werther's heart into bits so tid he knew the weight of waiting was all would sew it whole again. Her potent heartbreak lay stitched into a hideaway pocket like a packet of seeds. One day Werther would plant it and water it with tears. One day At would see the tree she could have climbed when still in its prime.

Long after Werther and At's decline, archaeologists will dig up the time capsule in a tin case and ponder Werther's At memories. Some poems, an unsent letter, unheard music: all would call tragically to future historians. Nothing, though, would be learned: Werthers would be Werthers and Ats, sadly, would be Ats.

Back to the Now-Now now, where Werther wanders numbly through the quantum foam. With no face, no cut of cake or dress to raise his hackles, he grows more conscious of his love's illiteracy. If suffering were only a job to do, Werther would be a rich man, but his fault led him to crack and shake in the worst poverty of all: tumbling towards a mirage, he'd let himself fall.

Now, begrudgingly, Werther watches At's wake unfold.

WHEN HE GOES TO LAY ROSES (AT'S FEET)

Lust's illusion lorded his senses broke: none sighted, none felt, he collapsed at her statue's foot. Desire, that busted consume of Parisian methods, horticultural brothels, pissoire handwashers, awaked.

Able-shaped plastic examples of food and fruit, rafts where pregnant worms flew, and bombwarnings: what you want, if you get it, might get *you*. Werther had stewed for two years how to get to At. Words untendered, music unspoken, bent grassblades threatened to unthirst his tongue's logic, make it freeze in midst of word neediness.

At's ears finally upon'd Werther's mouthglances, sprung potato eyes wide to burn, and wrapped in oven…foiled. There was where he failed—his words was no good for her. He thought after two years suffering for suffering's sake she'd beat up his longingbully with her kinfist, recognize him to be her One, but tides often change just when winds begin to blow, and boats fail to reason out of sinkmoat's sand.

Their Either/Or didn't connect themselves into an And. None to blame, but all the same, Werther's insides die. And At? At, visibly shook from her love's pawned rook, knew she'd acted bad, in spite of all her years. She'd seen Yes the Yesman gape in his jackblack's eye, but scratched and whipped it dead like a stick for hanging.

Just when she should have rubbed him with her medication something shook her and took her wind away. She'd seen, she knew, but for fear let him go. Oh At, why?

A MITE STUNT-SMOOCH
(NEGATED, TERSELY)

On his back, the Old Geezer was carrying his old memory house with a strap, a little white-dressed blixen adoor where his spinner once connected his jackblack, then still blooming with possibilities, such as chasing the friendly smell and smile of young red-haired blixens. They gave him more than just the time of day: those were the nights of soft vowels and no clocks.

The Old Geezer's life had been sketched in black and white before the killed-heart blues and hues were laid over. The fixers gave him a uniform to wear and worked him until he bent. The Old Geezer was a young Werther then, his smile pulled down by frownweight, the dark hair gone gray, shoulders that once pitched horseshoes now limp by his side.

Sin came out then to give his days a pressure worth bearing. There were so many blixens with sharing mines to boot: all seemed rosy until young Werther's page cracked and turned blue. He'd fallen into the hole, to the last a penchant for the bed where as a child he once dreamed and flew.

Now hugging the Big Nothing in the ground, tiredness waved over him anew: UnSin come to sing. Werther would go out and play if he could but wiggle his nose. The deathbird scene, though, for now just a dream—Werther's still sailing, still pailing words into his miserly house of memory.

Rest assured, the Old Geezer knows he hasn't been entirely UnWerther'd yet. Tired, yes, but unblixened, no: a fevered one just roosted into the room. Old Man Werther yet to be—now still young, see.

WAS SHE AT (OR NOWHERE?)

Werther, in his yearning search for At (though he hardly knew her yet as anywhere other than absence), had failed to take into account one fact: that he'd come full circle into a mode of cynical deadendedness, wherein he rounded cul de sacs forever, never scraping but the tires against the curb. From this unvantaged point of view, he was blind to the possibility of a high-riser.

He couldn't breathe amidst the altitudes of crazies. Too many of them interred the world with their unsavoriness. He knew, if nothing else, how hard it was to bring a world into his room that took the form of a saintly blixen. There was nothing but noise—he wintered without music, unattached.

Drawn from the stern gaggle of the bong he fixed his head with strong drinks and blixen dreams. Nowhere arrived every day, bigger than the moon, wider than the universe, stronger than any satyr. Dust blew and left unfixed the herald's eye. Somewhere, the lens of the moon showed pictures of the Earth to an audience of craters.

They fidgeted and sighed at the sight of such stark enjoiners, not believing their kin below was living so unloved. How far can you go before you want to turn back? Werther had gone so far as to be nearly gone, singing sins only in the shower, his thoughts burning, skewered, too tired to see the nude fertile sun.

THE MONDAY YOKE, TORN TWICE

Werther wandering seen strange things seething: a cripple felled himself against a glass door, a boy shot himself in the heart with a toy gun, a blixen in a bush tugged on a leash with a muskrat on the end. He sat by the pond edge singing to himself, thinking nothing was possible, wishing but not wishing he was elsewhere. Nothing came, nothing went.

At was nearby, but neither looked the other's way, strayed invisible to each other for another day. Werther would heave his thoughts in other directions, but At was on his mind. He didn't know otherwheres for his thoughts to be. He tried talking to a stray that let him rub its neck to backshivers. The little dog fell asleep. Three ducks flew past and shat.

The Wordikens, wizard-like gimlets uttered through a cow's mouth, ushered At into a dozen book's beginnings, but her story caved in on itself, left nothing there to read. At wondered where her Nextliness would come from. She didn't think she'd be able to buy a drink some nights, her spare pennies and nickels rolled end to end for food.

Just another day for the two spent wandering empties, a constant endingness planed on their wanings. At shrugged and read another book. Werther wandered. Nothing took. His heart jimmied now and then and shook. He knew the fever—she knew it too.

ROUGHLY (OR SO SPEAKING)

"It pushes the pushings out," At's Dad to BoatAt said, out cod hunting, the bay one big tear that day. At, mad at herself for letting Werther go unhooked, Away, Away, said: "What now Dad?" Dad, in his better days, could better the BigFish, but now he was not so new at the game and the old wind blew too hard for him to better his best.

Heartbreak had made him numb to wind and heartbreak—he lived a sober life now in a boat, in vitro no, but free, fed and warm. "What's important Dad?" At wanted to ask, but Dad's day is important, she sees, and shuts her trap which failed her so UnTraply back when it might've mattered—now Werther's in the ocean again, sigh.

Sunsparkles and flying fish on the gunwhales flapping their hellos to the two humans didn't merit At's attention. How can something let go, she thinks, catch me so off guard?

How can that man come in and go out of my life and still be so In? Back on land, Werther sat stone bench-like, awake but unaware, wondering: "Where do I belong?"

Inescapable sensations of UnNostalgia stuck lunglike to his medulla oblongata...a longing to be with At, the realization that At, for his intents and purposes (fifty wishes, fifty wishes...) no longer existed. There's slippage here, Werther thinks. Now I am not I, Atless. Not on her map, not on her ground. There had been an invasion, but nothing sweet to breathe was found.

DISTILLATION, I LAND (A SENSE)

At basked in resinous glory, but unrelated to a toned gate. She sewed her lapel patch up towards the mutton shop part of her heart: sheep knot to sheep knot. Fear stroked her tin pin moments before the gasplast's blast, but never in time of need did her fear level out.

Werther not that ably wrecked his own nick of time. The blixen didn't hatch his plan to bare, so much so his oxygen stitch caught fire and burned through every mask she could muster, except the last, the one that mattered most. Fear made her go away and fear made him follow—one's weakness another's strength—sun without moon, rain without bed.

A blixen's possible jackblack leaves, in the moment, ruin strewn where Werthers might have connected towards clemency of a different form, never a door slam, never a Bye-Bye, but chasing a permanent Now, furtive flowers grown Forever, or at least Ever and Ever, between two rocks.

At backed away from knowing a Now, but didn't know enough to let it hatch. She seemed to summon menace into everything good, and that was that. Blind, unable to see through to the other side where his warm arms made fate bend and cut out the cold, the unfeathered cold—she shivered end to end and knew why and of what she would die: loveless and luckless.

THE MAILMAN'S GOOD FOR A NOD
(when you're sinking by the side of the road)

At's basement window looked up at blue skybranches. She sat there stonily amongst her magazines and cigarettes glazing parrots for woodshop's songbird week. Now and then she thought about her man, his absence come out like a ghost to haunt her, her basement the wound she was trapped in.

"Quando quando quando:" the radio sung its smurk out. Her painted parrots smiled at her, eyes glazed-like on their mugs, but what a thing to be weaned on, a wooden bird, At thought. She licked her wounds as much as she liked them, aware of the Never Enough Fun that went around when the world filled itself with misery, everyone bucking towards sadness, pushing the bull fighter's joy pincers away.

Torn pantaloons and knickers strewn about the heater drying from morning dew, At rolled about the glade in joy, PURE joy, and poetry too. "Them bones gonna ride again!" she'd heard Werther sing. They was hand in hand, then. Not much of the day left to choose from. She sat around, thinking to climb up and get some blue sky emeralds. The days went round and round like a sawbuzz jail.

At snuggled herself to a squeezed quiet, numb to the world, numb to mind, numb to the number tree, money. Bills went unpaid for days, and days into weeks. The world was lacking charity. At lived in hope, though hope had been taking her again and again to the drink, furthering her away from her why in the world: "Werther why don't you come and be Blixened now, huh?"

FIXIN TO BE BLIXENED, WICK

Werther had gone wandering amidst the steam and green of a small prestigious school where studies ranged from bad to better but the social life was good. He sat staring from a bench at the near distant range, one of a few mountain ranges running east to west instead of north to south, and saw a most beautiful woman walking with her parents.

Mom and Dad didn't see their eyes meet, didn't see the gauzed gaze of knowing come unveiled almost into smiles. Werther wondered if they'd ever meet again, looking at the back of her long black curls. In the library he hoped to see her again. He went and went but she never came to study. Books upon books fell into his lap.

His lust eventually fell into a nap and envisioned clear and what,since a dream, could be called true, an image of their liking each other's points of view, lasting not an eternity, but close, a good tenure, better than most. But, since a dream, he awakened to trudge home.

The last night of term came with a passed hand, as if some creator had waved his No-No thing over the string continuum that ended abruptly without a connection. As if, then, insult from the jury, Werther was condemned to view his beauty pulling away from the curb in Dad's van for another misery summer at home, in prison, UnWerthered.

SEVEN SENSES FOR AT

Werther lathered and shaved but didn't bite the shadow away. His tattered sleeves were come undone and made plain obvious the nature of his rust. He'd walked all day with pictures of At in his rainback. Every time he opened his bag her ocean lapped against his ears, glowing green and red orange waves from longing's black black sea. Werther was curious then to know her cobblestone streets and wheatfields, see.

In his dingy room, no, not dingy, merely Atless, he tried her pictures come to life, but eyes looked down and away. He spun weightless in the dark grip of many iron circles locked round his jackblack's cave. Even music and infinity failed to fill and spin his senses away from their unevenness.

"Wake up, wake up," she called from far away in his mind, a daydream come to life. He imagined meeting her in the forest where trees watched and waited for them to Werther-At themselves free. Could he fit her world into his abundant worldlessness?

He wondered if his blue and her blue would mix into trueblue. Her songs and silent gestures was where he wanted to be. At, he thought, be At to me, your songs with mine, entwined.

KIN TO EYES, ABOARD (PIER)

Half asleep, Werther's guardian Cababel sang: "the maw that coasts choose to be together around the near brick of distratocaster…" "No mute sounds pass to keyhole grasps where ice sinks into mink-lined mirrors of play, or what…placelessness?" "Further on is the point to be, laced up to a knee, the elbow's cousin, where we learn to think things out roundly."

"Were we to ask questions of fate, would The Fate Lady answer? Or would she blame The Sand Man for not being a heroine addict? Some blixens only want hardened criminals, the kind with visible scars and gas-soaked insides unlevied from moorings, held together by one bolt."

"Can't blame a blixen for bad taste, but what about blindness? Pint after pint can shave away near any foggy bitterness, but the sorry lioness straights her fearful arrows into undignitied songlungs when absence of foresight rises." "Choices at the end of the line: soft splash into warm water, or The Big Cold Dive into shocktroop's unloved leathers." "You ever thought why love songs leave you untouched? Used to feeling bad deeply, how would you know otherwise?

Simpler to say: I want to make you crazy, say your name, turn you into something you wouldn't believe." "Simpler to say: thatched roof above your dead bed lets in both rain and light. Decide which you like." "Simpler to say: let a crazy one into the room—they understand me." Werther opened his eyes just as Cababel's song faded, its final phrase stuck in a groove he understood he was meant to pursue.

BOOKS REDDER LICKED AT (UNBIBLED)

It's an eternal 3 a.m.: clocks tick to shudders, lidded shutters clamped, unprovoked by desire's haunted lamp. Werther wanted to ask them all: are you Angel or Devil, tapped? Before pissing another temporary detour through eternal hell, his breath rising through steam and perk of fogbird, he sad-guitared At's departure from his illusion's tense: not future, not past, not present, At.

Maybe he'd waited too long to act against his lethargy. By the time he'd had the courage she was in love with another. She tried by blackjack jury to fit him into her correspondence. There was no way, though, not even a one-way street of distractions.

That morning when he woke he noticed even his bed was sick. He'd been dying instead of rising to cockcrow's dare. He vowed to never leave the house again without vowing to be alive. "Pure poetry exists off the page, in life," he said. Then a new one come to remind his books of their demise.

She fathomed a funny liking to him out of the blue. Werther was stunned at first to find himself on duty. This blixen pryed open his rusty door and hopped in smiling. Words failed him again, so he didn't speak, just opened his mouth to her kiss. Her hand traced scimitars across his chest. He bled, was alive. Red flowers rose to be heard and warmed the air like an orange sun's peel.

All of his Nothing changed with a day's drive to a lake, to a tree, to an open field. She was the leader of her childhood gang and showed him the forest's door. Hand in hand, they walked through. Calm water lapped against the shore. They threw their stone in.

WERTHER DREAMING AT

His jackblack had tasted her fume for two days ungunned. Logic in that, there was, a clearing dream again, without fear, thirst, or desire. Werther's hungry lack craved her comings and goings. At, on the other end of his desire, stayed fast: no knickers blew in the wind no hand extended in the arbor moon.

She'd gone away, flown on a plane across an ocean, thrown a dirigible span as the wrench to twist Werther's back into wreckage, undecorated by love ribbons, and worse, scratched barbs thrown to make him stop thinking of her. Now he began his days and nights in the desert, whispering At's name atop monk burial grounds.

"Should've win'd her, should've win'd her," the seafaring ghosts of his ancestry insisted, "should've thrown yourself in the water and drowned instead of trying to learn to swim in her uncharted currents." They laughed at Werther, hammered with woodspoons against the gunwales of his death ship, set sail one night in the sea of his sleep. They laughed, the dead, amused by the antics of one so alive but living so unworthily.

All was fog and seaweed. At was shrouded in a distance yet to be imagined. Maybe there was no place for her in Werther's jackblack, his crowned head's tool case in need of a shed to fill with other new chances to take before At's scaffold could be built to breach her parapet. Werther wakes, his eyes open but blind to daylight's mercy. Merciless, the day is night. Atless, Werther is *not*.

BASEMENTED IN (TO THE GRIND)

Creation is often born of a sickness, Werther thought. He sighed, wanted to sigh into a microphone, wanted to sigh so loud and long that At would shudder, shiver, look up from her down-den and fall into retrospective love. No. Not like that. Werther'd grown used to existing with futility, like an old ochre sweater someone died in that fit just right.

At may have been his once in some other zone. Werther cursed this reality that kept them apart. Worse yet was knowing that he'd stumbled and failed to follow the line At had drawn in the sand for him to cross. She was turtle eggs, she was ostrich plumes, she was the Big Now, but No had shook its fist, and that was that.

He tried to swallow his tongue, tried to hold his breath, even tried to speak, but nothing worked. He stared into space, wondering nothing but At's face into a smile of Yes-Eyes. Werther couldn't stand the thought of committing himself to a genre, but with a rare glimpse of clearsight he saw he'd tripped into the lowliest construct of all.

He understood the blues AND knew nothing, both. Nothing was the best and worst of everything. There were shoes for him to roam. There was a woman made for him, but a big what if crept tighter around his mind: what if there was nowhere but At?

Werther fell into his head. Now he was lost. Now there was only No and Nothing, and even thinking led Nowhere. He was washed ashore, naked.

TOO BUSY BEING WERTHER
TO BE WERTHER

Time for a new good luck pen, Werther thought, dribbling ink across torn restaurant checks. He'd gone to think maybe he'd finally come undone for good from At's negating response, thought maybe now he could come face to face with her in a crowded room and not fall down in a piled heart, thought maybe he wouldn't die, wouldn't cry for her song, would live with someone else in mind.

In the past few days he'd kissed new lips that wanted his lips to be hers—he'd held, slow-danced with, cherished the hours of mercy granted from above or beyond, wherever the chain of command assembled to decide who lived in heaven and who lived in hell with no mercy to breathe for oxygen. There was hope. Or was there?

Those new kisses grew stale fast and made Werther fall into a deep despair that was deeper than the last. Then he had a good day, walking in quiet snow, completing tasks, staring at faces and reflections, but when he realized near five that he'd had a good day all to himself, Werther suffered through the harshest five-second despair of all and briefly cried out against the oncoming night. Winter, he could do. It had felt like winter through all his days, but night, he thought, pray for me someone that I survive.

BACK TO AT (A TREMBLOR)

In a rainstorm Werther rode his bike as if on a lonely river log. He'd dropped his broken umbrella miles ago, didn't mind getting wet, but didn't like not having At to smile dry with. He knew life had a way of taking peculiar turns. Too bad, though, his road had been so straight and narrow, with so many cold wrecks left behind to sift through. Late at night he came across another unmade memory: At.

Her face in every tree, her voice in every puddle, her earthquakes shook his ground without apology. How simple life becomes, Werther thought, once you fall into the ocean and don't care how deep you go. This before realizing he wanted to see the surface many more times before going down for good. Still, Werther found himself undone, drowning.

There was no way around it. Werther had created a moon for At to set down, but his craters somehow unmade her and she hurtled away into thrown-away space and time. Werther didn't know, of course, that she was as lost as he, far away, floundering in her Wertherless misery. Suffering without meaning, she thought, is meaningless. Wertherless, she felt herself half a woman, unholy.

Werther would crawl through glass and blood to alter At from statue to human form. He'd turn her slow like clay, let her rise naturally from the ground. It's not that life is hard, he thought, but leaping into life that scares people. To feel alive is terrifying and new, he wanted to tell At, because we're used to being dead. At was getting the drift, finally, and called out Werther's name.

BOOK THREE: MISCELLANY

"Fishponds and a madman's honey…"

--Wire, "Madman's Honey"

WOODCHOPPERS (DAWN'S EARLY LIGHT)

Two stone lions wrapped in plastic framed the door. Golfers begged for sunset's Zen. Hills beckoned behind the red flag's floor. The big double-barreled tree reached for becomes a lecture none of whose words ring true to the uninspired. Their clubstrokes went astray. All appeared to be lost, so they stopped keeping score and began to explore pure form. Werther hit two balls into the water. Coin gave up after seven.

"The mind freed from world is the world of mine," Werther said before thwacking his ball into the forest. Later, the golfers toted bottled beer & snack foods forth. White doves descended to the green for crumbs, and the sun began to sag. Coin pointed and said, "Don't you want the little red flag, don't you want it?" Werther thought of his hot-blooded Mediterranean woman standing next to the flag, waving him on.

At waited elsewhere, in wings far from the green, further still from any green-induced calm. Where she wanted to be she wasn't being, and where she was she wasted days without trying. No use fetching eggs you'll never fry. The farmer and golfer live day to day. She, though, failed to see the light at the end of the fairway.

The golfers slept between each bad shot. Walking their clubs to the next disaster, they dreamed of satisfactory outcomes, unmissed chances to par, to eagle—the next green, always the next green. At, in her sleep, dreamed of other places putters couldn't take her to slake the thirst, the hungry thirst for an end that does not hurt.

YOUNG MAY KNOT (SATELLITE DISH)

Werther's nursery rhyme opened beer can-like, a popped top shed to bare its yellow sea-foam lake. He smiled to feel the amber glow burrow into his bones and raise his hopes level with the shore. He desired change, not another long summer, not sand-filled shoes emptied on the kitchen floor, not pondering with glass his magnified handful world, finding rock after rock, all different inside.

In May, everything bloomed into green light and pink, promising to warm the winter's scarred heart, scared away from living by icicle daggers, heated to blast-furnace degrees, burning sacred books unshirting all possibility.

Fortune cookies, the first sled of truth, keyed into the Ching his I squinted through, hoping the words received were dishes of fruitful knowledge ripening into full-whispered flowers, lips glistening with beads of whiskey, vodka, and gin, numbed by kiss's rub, lip to lip, cheek to cheek, and vice versa.

The moth train rounded its curve, sounds its three a.m. arrival with chant of horn and track trundle. Sneaking past some nights seven cars short without stopping, it hurried elsewhere since no one seemed to be hurrying away, just digging in deeper for the big blow to come, some of them convinced they were in heaven, others in hell, while Werther thought most would agree that where we are doesn't matter—we're all going nowhere, eventually, fast.

ORANGE GROVE IN A FUNHOUSE MIRROR

No use flogging the rice paper wall with your mute, Werther thought. The sentries at the gate will prevent your escape. But so what, you never wanted to leave the frenzy of the beehive, you only wanted to get some air and perspective on the size of your box's bees. So many before you made the mistake of accepting too soon the false security offered by a fearful mate.

Their cowardice will keep you down: you'll go nowhere while the world tosses in its quantum foam, a blue and white tomato, an ocean of black lettuce. The sun is acres away, but you are always thinking of its heat, its potential to devour even the most giant of its companions, if only given the chance. Like the young who seem old, the sun wrinkles and winks.

Your flight is marred by constant turbulence. You were never far from your seat for long. The sun wore you down—those who called you poet were liars, and those who called you liar were cheats. What difference did it make? You were alive, untamed and free: they couldn't tie you down to kill you. All at once there was little all at once left.

Werther's lips smacked their bits of bad honey. He thirsted for vinegar rather than suffering the uncharmed lips of attempted sweetness. Love, like everything else, was a construct of the senses, and learning to kick and scream was all that kept him sane. A tribe of mad monks and poets swarmed around his boat. They were not cannibals and he had no fear when he fell into their jungle.

A RUSTING HULK (HUSKLESS)

A Jim Beam and Coke dusted the bartop. Droplets were sucked through straws by penniless nightcrawlers, not carrion, but carrying on, or attempting to at least keep things going. A jukebox neon glow bathed the willing in light the color of mercy, if mercy was a living scarf.

Spotted dogs waited near the door, scratching claws against pavement, waiting to follow the stranger home, waiting to surprise the drunk's reverie while navigating firefly roads. Stone is a constant. So is whiskey once arrived at. The night's walk to nowhere goes cemetery-wise. One more drink would have made the eyes forget to see.

Drunk Werther wandered amongst moon gray headstones, respectful but diligently insisting, "I'm alive. You're not." Finger pointing to moon, star, and sky—dog howl's howl to crawl and cry—a craving for morning, welcome and light, warming the mind to the idea of life.

Two new ghosts on grave's hill, locked arm in arm, fighting for one more spell of sense, one more marriage of felt and fern, grass blades bent to make the cut. The happy drunk becomes a sad drunk, and seeing ghosts Werther ran home, to weep, to sleep, to wake again and find his own.

A CLOCKLESS SHIFT (UNTIMELY FALL)

Werther had a raccoon treed sublimely last night up branches and bark, and raised his shotgun upwards of heaven where the critter, soon to be a soul, eyed him warily. "You're smart to run all your life, he told it, but now you're dead." Something sighed inside. Werther lowered the gun and let it go. "What's one more trash can tumbled, one more turnip gone from the garden when coons must get sad too?"

And now he was flushing his brains out onto the tracks through a gap in the underdress of a jiggling crazy train. Two men across from him spoke on the subject of pancakes: both like them on the small side. The talk turns to cheese: "I'm not much of a cheese connoisseur," one said, "I'm a Cheez WHIZ connoisseur." They both laughed.

The train started up again after taking on new souls. They're going nowhere, or at least it feels that way. Werther's thoughts wander. He's going home but there will be no one there to welcome him. He thinks of staying on. The mail can be forwarded, bills can be paid from afar. "You either go until you stop or never stop going. At the same time you get there either way."

The man behind Werther burps, excuses himself. His wife burps, says nothing. In the foreign city Werther saw couples hand in hand, but no eyes looked at his with the intention of locking. "Some trips show you there's no place to go back. Other trips make you wish you'd never left."

MOLLY'S UDDER, UTTERED MOLLY

Butter kept her busy.
The seasons were few.
Lost kites never returned.

ELIAB'S GRAVE (BUTTERCUPS)

Tonight Werther felt like loving, like clapping his thigh-hands against her thigh-hands, like seeing curves see themselves as illusions into which they bend and refract without breaking, like ripping grass from the earth to become chattle, to chattle and prattle until dawn.

He must have hallucinated the day, its beaded-damp hairs, its denial of yesterday, its unforgiving rejection of headless mops. Werther spoke with no one, saw many, but none revealed themselves to be searching for any core. A volcano smolders inside while it waits to explode, one day becoming an island people pay to see, but in the meantime…

She comes to unsettle his universe with gravel. She whispers bicycle tires rubbing against spoke legs. His knees are ripped, though, when the stick is thrown in to make him fall. She is the dust of a dirt road, the speed of the highway, the plunge into a bridgeless ravine, and he goes crashing willingly into her machine.

"I can go home now," he thinks, "the night is done like a cake that must wait until morning to be frosted." Last night lifted the veil, found them shy but unblinking. Still drunk on her sweet wine, Werther waited for the headache. What had his whiskey done? A taste made her want more.

SIX: SOUFFLES

RAIN, ALONE UNTIL

I've seen, finally, the yellow pear in an early morning light. In Helsinki, a taxi was left running in front of the botanical gardens, its driver an eager philatelist out to authenticate a stamp's reproduction of his favorite flower. Our dreams take us to strange places. We wait for days to arrive that never end. One day we'll record these dreams and watch them later. It goes without saying that the future is soon to be.

She led me by the hand to see the old shaman who lived in the hills. He had learned to rig the television so his dreams could be seen by children from surrounding villages. My eyes had failed me. My heart kept on, but why, or for what, or for a book I will one day write, I do not know. She danced around me. My friends were open doors with arms stretched out. My friends were love songs, but I was senseless. She was my arm in arm girl, leading me back to the world. Where had I been all those years? Heartbreak City.

We called out to you. We wanted you to leave your stone age behind. We wanted you to learn a new language, to escape the cave or at least bring your cave habits out into the open. There were five doors to choose from, delicacies behind each, things that tasted and things with no taste. Strings echoed through your mind. You paced a room, wanting to call someone, but there was no one to call. Crickets chirped. A stair creaked. The future began to move in your direction.

Metaphor began to take shape, to become real. You saw the emptiness between words. You saw how to fill those spaces with meaning. Metaphor was the cement. Words were the bricks. Your lips twitched for no reason. How would you be judged? No one knew the truth and you were remote even from yourself. Finally you achieved two levels of meaning with everything you said, but you were the only one who noticed. Someone turned on a radio. Static was a metaphor for music.

I could have an appointment tomorrow, the string that turns on the light, the train that waits, the door that opens but never shuts. I could meet someone tomorrow, be brave and say what I'm thinking, or write in a different notebook, the unlined page, the unkissed lip, the talk without talk, the hopeless hope. I could twist a tree into a fig, a fish into a light bulb, a future into a past. I could try to keep all the long walks home alone out of mind until the train leaves from the station.

When we crossed the desert we were magenta with sand. Don't leave us so alone with our thoughts. These urns come wrapped in gold cotton. Silver batteries fed the video static. We were at the feet of marching mountains. Our writers were shot by machines. Death was an empty heart. We were addicted to images. At the same time, we were a dark-haired girl with green eyes who never said the world was going to end.

Absence filled much of your time. You were always a guest on someone else's couch. We were little things, subtle gestures of mercy, silver cigarette cases, two lucky stones, pens and pencils that felt good to write with, a letter from a friend in another country. There were obstacles as well, broken shoelaces, leather that cracked and split, days you didn't feel like working when play was no fun either. You slept a lot, and we watched you.

This beginning has many ends. The new key to the new place comes with a last look at the old place and the handing over of the key. The new street brings a new face that looks like a face you once wanted to know but failed to meet. The mind roams where the body cannot. Weighed down by memory, the mind continues its journey, always looking ahead while always looking back.

He was a waiter in a busy restaurant. Even there, in the midst the restaurant's hustle and bustle, he sometimes felt alone. The world is a construct of illusions, he thought, nothing in the middle of the big everything. Sometimes he stopped what he was doing to look around and felt that none of it was real. After his shift, he went to a bar and was surrounded by others in search of wisdom and company and euphoria. If there were poems on beer bottles, he thought, then perhaps things would be different. The river would flow and power the machine. He went home, slept, and lived in a dream.

There were differences to be noted, always an accounting of things to be done. In one town you could see the Milky Way. In another, trains that left on time arrived late to their destinations and seeds planted in rich soil didn't always grow to be trees. There is no worse way of going to bed than knowing the last words out of your mouth before sleep were wrong and that being drunk or a poet was no excuse.

He felt like something was beginning, that something was happening. Words were being used, trying to figure themselves out, trying to find their way home. Once upon a time, they might say, there was a something or a someone. For now, they were content to just slant and dance across the page. He knew something was up but that he would have to wait a while longer to see what it was.

He left the Palais Des Beaux Arts, where he frequently went to look at the Magrittes. A model was being photographed next to the tram stop. He leaned against the base of a statue and watched her until his tram arrived. He wondered if he would ever see her picture in a magazine. As the tram pulled away, she looked up at him and smiled.

Later that night, he fell asleep with her on his mind, and when he woke up the next day, he was still thinking about her and wondered who she was. Everything seemed unreal and far away. He listened to the radio and looked out at the gray Belgian sky. He wondered what she was doing at that exact moment.

He went for a walk in the forest and saw a deer. The deer disappeared into a dark part of the woods. A few days later, after finishing his shift, he was having a beer by himself in a hotel bar when she walked in. She looked at him and smiled when she recognized him from the tram. His heart pounded at first until he realized the moment was real. She lived in Paris and had been staying in the hotel for several weeks while working in Brussels. They drank wine, talked, and told stories about their lives. When the bar closed, they went up to her room and lay awake with each other until the sun started to rise. Somewhere else in the city, the tram driver was waking up and getting ready for work.

The wolf is never wrong or right. The sheep is never wrong or right. There are ways in and ways out of every situation. Everyone is a hunter. Everything is both real and allegorical at the same time. Metaphors melt into meat. Flesh is eaten. One small victory is enough when a scream has gone unchecked for years. Don't be afraid, little sister, have no fear. The maze is not a maze. Look at it from above, it's simple. Follow me, I'll take you there. Let's be drunk. You look beautiful today.

All the clues have been handed over. How fast it happened. This day was more than just a day. Everything all at once is how a tree thinks when it's lived for a long time. The house is a mind. Elsewhere in the city, mussels are being served with bread and pommes frites. Tall yards of beer are being drunk by old men who sit and stare through cafe windows as the world passes by. The moon smiles and winks.

Tuning in a radio late at night, there were short bursts of sound from other countries. Voices. Words. Separate realities. Satellites circled the Earth. A voice broke through, the voice of the beehive. It was too far away to be heard and receded like a wave back into chaos, except for a few small fragments that made it into their dreams.

The story keeps coming apart. It doesn't want to hold. More important things enter the mind. Phone calls need to be made, bills paid. It doesn't matter that the story won't hold. Pictures are more important than words. Is that true? Somewhere in time this is being written, unfolded in front of silent eyes looking for words worth repeating.

The night was warm enough to leave the windows open. Curtains slow danced with the breeze. It was *the* this and *the* that and you were either too tired to cross out your *ands* or too miserable to re-read your sentences. Stories played themselves out in your mind but you were too lazy to write them down. Silly people all around, they came and went, but you were neither rock in the stream nor wolf in the weeds. Another house, another day, another mark on the wall.

We're not sure where the road will take you but it will bring you in from the cold and make you want to stay warm. The stars will glitter favorably above your nights. Orion leans against the hill's horizon. There are ways to understand the maze.

Men are desperate creatures, she thought, but their desperation is beautiful and leads to many things, it creates options and destroys walls. The more desperate, the more extreme their mad acts and truths. She was sitting at a cafe table, thinking about him. Something has changed, she thought. No more walks in the dark. She wrote a poem, she tore up a poem. She wanted to talk to him and not write. Her thoughts were bricks holding open the door of possibility.

She of the eye that looked, she of the knowing that knows. She who said my name without fear, she who called out in the night, she whose whisper put me to sleep and keeps me warm. She of the white cloud, she who opened the door, she who is no longer hidden.

Those books on the wall are distractions. The ice on the window means nothing. There's only one warm body here, mine. The blankets are soft. There is nothing on the walls. I'm going to think but I'm not going to speak. I realize I will one day run out of things to say and that if I'm lucky I'll stop thinking soon too. Are you silk, or sick? Snow is on its way. Come here and stay warm.

He thinks about the stars above. Mistakes made in the past sometimes lead to victories in the future. Safe houses can't be bought, he thought, but they can be borrowed. He ordered another beer. She put her arm through his and pulled him in.

I wanted to be heard. I wanted people to listen until they wondered what I was going to say next. The songs came from far away. I was screaming all the time. Life was plot, but the page didn't demand that I look at the page, it demanded that I look at the world. I am the circle in the flame. I am the branch of the flowering tree, the missing link. I am the garden, the ember, the polygraph test of the heart.

This story began in antiquity, before the first sleep. It said: suppose this story, suppose these words. Something was stirred. There was reason to believe that words could change reality, the way sex and sleep brings two strangers together. Sometimes it's primitive. Sometimes angelic. People walk the streets, thinking. Fiction, reality, construct. Awareness trying to break through. Deprivation of the senses. Light through water. A voice trying to break through, or many voices, many stories. Fragments. Puzzles. Pie. Or a pincushion's cousin.

Sunrise over the hills to the east. Railroad tracks leading south and north. Fireflies in the yard, an empty birdhouse. The way she moves, the way she smiles. The painting on the wall, the broken stove, the low stone wall. There will be snow on the ground soon. Somewhere, the two of them begin their day. We wandered alone in the rain, looking for others wandering alone in the rain.

A door opened to a tunnel. We stepped inside. The door closed behind us.

GREEN CLOWN ON A BLACK CROSS

"Sufferation of solitude and place! You were a flier in silver-gray shawls, simile of storm-anger. 'Whose clansman are you?' they ask, and you answer: 'I am of the race of heaven.'"

--Velimir Khlebnikov

1.

I was balanced on the blueswing of an oxen's sadstained tin globe, its bambootrigger shacks and hovels collapsed beneath the weight of an eerily-eared monkey's disaster. Not that the night had given up on me, no, nothing like that, but I was not about to leave the house to go searching for my Katya's lost braid, last seen slithering into the swampy murk beneath city hall's trampled felt lion's feet.

2.

I fell spittle-shingled into the exploding fountain's metallic grasp. Its shacklehand's grip went unletup until I released the hopesong from my heart: swimming stream of built-up, pent-in implosive love: tears, rash, delirium, dystended sense of time, an abundant awareness of unreality, odd hungers that I foolishly held on to the way a dancing horse keeps time with its hoof to the beat of a Roman mazurka.

3.

My ship landed in a soft patch of grass. We celebrated our arrival with aquamarine glasses of wurn. Oftentimes we spoke of past glories: "I will fly, I will beckon the mothership home: we will dance around the flymozzled offal cloud in the shimmying yellow of the sun-nickel's eye. No ghosts, no darkness, no fear. In their place, the cold liquid metal of featherlight caresses: chills in the spine, chills in the head!"

4.

We discovered once again that we have great difficulties in trying to understand one another. Similar problems once existed between the sloths and the lowly mink, but look how they have resolved their configuration of malaise and mutual neglect! Let us learn from their heartwarming tale, let us celebrate with a pint of winter ale in the garden's glassed-in tavern.

5.

The Kiblingers exchanged glances with The Mohair Unit. Too early to predict whether or not there would be full cooperation between the deckhands and the upwardly-mobile floribunda. The strength of their sneezes toppled all our cardhouses from miles away as we observed through telescopes from the perch of our specially-equipped yellow and white striped field tent.

We saw a man die of his own laughter, we saw airships flown by hyena-faced wolves in penguin suits. Later that day, our post was recalled to the rear and I never saw such strange beauty again. That is why I am making this voyage now: to finish the lexigraphical accompaniment to my modest tome.

6.

That night, we ate thin yellow pancakes weighed down with dollups of sweet sour cream and apricot jam, sprinkled over with a brief flurry of powdered sugar. Uncle Victor laughed so loud that his glass eye popped out of his head and landed in the butter. Professor Volkov had a thought: "One day, talented meaniemen will build a mother ship, travel backwards in time, and fool us all into submission. What will happen then?"

He licked his jam-dipped spoon and lifted a steaming cup of coffee to trembling lips. We looked at him and sensed that he was afraid, a fact that did not make any of us feel good. Still, I asked for another pancake and licked my plate clean in the kitchen when I was done. One last cookie, then it was off to bed.

7.

The Republicans moved in on the small enclosure of resistance fighters with a battalion of yawning tanks looking to make quick meat of the well-trained but misled intelligentsia. The tanks were stenciled with white letters that said: "Nowhere is safe." Flamethrowers prepared to spit their juices over the heads and upturned faces of these poor, waylaid children.

A sun of unrecognizable hue cast an indifferent raygaze over the pock-marked planet. Its blind eye the moon opened its torn limp lid with the rehabilitated horns of ostrich nerves. There was the moon's first love, the Earth! She hung in her silk hammock from a hook at the edge of the universe. The moon cried an ecstatic's tear. Torn sheet screams ripped from the blowhole of its mouth. The Earth rocked gently in her netswing and wiggled shakerattle toes against the chill of the lonely solar wind.

8.

So many things had been written about the author's agitation, his lethargy, his careless and partial preoccupation with detail. That winter, late at night, he often opened his eyes and thought: "I don't care about anything." In fact, all the author cared about was love. Meanwhile, in a space station far above the Earth, Volkov floated awake in his sleeping pouch, stricken with insomnia and a desire to tramp through snow with big boots on his feet and a bottle of vodka in his hands.

He listened to the snores of the other crew members and thought about his Katya, picking black currants near their stream for pies to be eaten on the porch swing at sunset, the sound of crickets in the air, heat lightning in the sky. Volkov missed the Earth. He missed his Katya and everything he was unable to be near. There was nothing he could do about his longing, though, so he closed his eyes and waited for sleep.

9.

A silver ring sleeps beneath moon-glowing snow. A repairman emerged from the heating duct. "Here's the problem." he said, holding up a rabbit's head the size of a ripe autumn cabbage. "No wonder you've been cold." Volkov's cousin Pasha shivered and said, "Well, at least from now on..."

She wanted the duct man to leave soon. Any moment now Capstan would arrive. She wanted to be his first impression when he entered the room, not this unwholesome brute in damp green overalls, the smell of old garlic seeping from every one of his pores like squid oozing through pearl-illuminated coral reefs.

10.

"Am I a scientist or an artist?" she thought to herself. The duct man burped in the kitchen and emerged with the rabbit head in a clear plastic bag. "Bowling," he said. Pasha paid him in cash and opened the door. "Be seeing you," she said, and: "By the way, what were the rabbit's last thoughts?" The duct man turned, held the bag level with his eyes and said, "Homesickness, or perhaps jealousy."

Pasha closed the door and turned to face her apartment. It was one of those moments where, without any extreme gestures to provoke an alchemical change in behavior, Pasha knew that everything had changed, nothing would ever be the same again: he would never love her, there would never be an identifiable moment of contentment for the rest of her life. "No, no," she told herself, "Don't collapse like a fallen lung or a failed souffle."

Cicadas hummed on the balcony and tapped against the window. Warm Santa Ana winds blew through the olive trees. A coyote padded silently down the middle of the early morning street, before dawn, before the first day of real tribulation.

11.

I am the harem of rage. I am the moon's lost side, fountains dotting my two platters like gold leaf leftovers fallen to the herbalist's sawdust floor. Okay, none of that. I am the mailman, here is your mail, good day. The butcher is of heartier stock than I, but I am the mailman. Are you waiting for a letter? I will deliver it, not he, not the butcher. He's only good for meat. The letters I bring offer so much more in the way of visceral entertainment, vicarious extravagances. I know because I peek. You people are naughty, naughty, naughty. I'll finger you, dirty pricks and dishes all.

12.

The Doctor: "Men and women of Mars, why do you still hide from us? Did Viking frighten you?" Mother Of All Battles, I miss you. Things are tough here too. There are Texans at every turn. The Alamo is not history. Now for an infusion of fresh plasma: we squandered a huge lead, we fumbled the ball.

Lost in small Belgian villages, we looked at maps beneath a gray ceiling of sky. For three days running, we forgot our brothers and sisters in space, on other planets hurdling through the universe. How could we forget our extended family? But we did. Our own spaceship refused to fly. No way to repair it here on Earth. We are stranded.

A.

A book blown open by the wind, a symphony in the hand: crosscurrents of dreams revolve around the battery, the empty page, the blank tape, nothing. At the trial, a final battle for the right to exist, beg the jury to mark their ballots with an A.; absolve the accused: anno Domini, anno mundi, ante meridium, artium magister.

A. is an unknown quantity, therefore, related to Z. Accept him. Comply. He is more than a simple equation, a symbol for nothing. Give him a good grade, an A in History, if it pleases you to please him. He aspires to amend the abyss of his coma in Africa.

Sleeping late, staying up all night, were ultimately tedious. On the island, where there was no routine to speak of, a traveler noted A.'s volcanic nature and told him he resembled an aa' that had hardened but still boiled inside. A. thanked the traveler and placed a wreath of aal around his neck, for which he said they must liquefy their pact with a glass or two of the local vintage.

"How much can you drink?" the host asked.

"Forty-seven aams," the traveler joked. They drank, and in their hallucinations became the creatures they had always been without revealing their disguises: Aardvark, earthpig, Orycteropus capensis. There were times when A. was not quite himself. When he spoke of the ordeal of existence, they dismissed him as being abundantly Aaronical. He ignored their taunting jealousies and planted an Aaron's rod, adding a touch of the serpent his presence so often implied to those who knew him only metaphorically.

He was never abducted from Away Down From. He denied the rumors that he had lived a third life from the month of Ab. He never knowingly ate alabamine, the abbreviation of which preceded C. in the river upon which all solids floated. Mustafa urged him to take alba from the shelf: "The Chillish winds have been summoned."

"Absurdo!" A. yelled, "They're Santa Ana winds, not Chillish."

"When we have smoked the abaca you will change your mind," Mustafa said.

"I was there when they abacinated Riley's eyes," A. said. "I understand and am thoroughly versed in discomforting thoughts and actions. Abacination hurts."

"No kidding." Mustafa agreed.

A.'s foot fell asleep. It reminded him of the tedious troweling when they laid the abaciscus at the Parthenon. Maybe it had been elsewhere. He was forgetful, had seen too much and was blind to the order of things. He needed an abacist to keep track of events, places, people, things...the stuff dreams tended to pass over in favor of juicier fixings.

The ship's sails were taken aback by the wind of cliches and parametrical devices. You could not say that he was abactinal, for he was not a radiate animal. In the fifth century he specialized in the abaction. He was the kind of abacter who enjoyed the splash he often made at weddings. He was neither polygamous nor a talkative disc jockey.

The abaculus had nothing to do with Mozart's virtuosity, but everything to do with a stiff neck at the coliseum.

He knew three girls: Tusca, Dori, and Ion. They begat him children and those children begat him grandchildren. He gave them numbers instead of names, which saved money and speaking oxygen. You must be patient with him, for he will refer you to the painless solution to all your difficulties. You won't be pleased, perhaps, but you will be relieved, sleep well, and think: "Ah, that's it, then. Big deal and goose bumps in a cherry pie for tarty brats in the belfry."

Bear with them, further the nest's warmth. Seize the pickled herring. A case a day that ends in nonsense is cheaper than a full head of ideal lettuce dropped in the sewer. Wash the dirt off, continue on your way. You have heard of days like this before. Be careful now. There are holes in the walls through which prying eyes stop and stare and know that you don't know you're being watched. In the darkness, you will not see the hands reach for you until it is too late. And then you fall, irreversibly and uncontrollably, down through Abaddon's open jaws, abaft the beam where you balanced. There is nothing in the void except to comply to the laws of abaissance. It is dark in the bottomless pit, forever; it is abaiser.

An interesting story was in the paper, a strange odor in the air, abalienating three of our fellow citizens, who made off with the loot that fell from an armored car's open door. Descriptions were given, drawings circulated. No one escaped; everyone was abalienated in their abalienation. They'll wait for you at home if you have no plan but to take the money and run.

He was eating fresh abalone at a restaurant in Santa Cruz. The food had been certified at three abamperes. Abandoned now before you reach the living edge, you know and understand meanings before they have been employed. You are wholly abandoned when the stone is cut out. You lose your character, your depth, your honesty. A. will care for the abundum in your absence. Don't thank the judge who sentenced you; enjoy the abonnition. The abastiston has nothing to do with your own trepaning. You were sentenced to be pinned down; the judge still enjoys his abarticulation.

"The prisoner was abased," Mofo revealed.

"Tongues opened stairways to proclaim abasement," Colly remembered.

Mofo: "Does nothing leave you feeling abashed?"

Colly: "Nothing." She answered everything before thinking. Hence, false data poured from the lab: premature conclusions, dead judgments, yellow thoughts. She rolled in abashment, the individual fully uncreated, compressed abasia with no lack of Persian coins, abassis.

"Except your abatable critiques," Colly said, abating Mofo's attempted abatement of snapped character traits.

"A declaration of war, love," Mofo warned, "I'm piling the abattis." A shadow passed over the abatjour. They looked skyward. The symphony faded momentarily. Mofo tapped the A batteries, cleared the static, eliminated the power surge. "Have you ever toured an abattoir?" Colly asked, a reflection of the music in her voice.

Mofo: "I once followed the abature to recreate the fox's panicked last moments. It can't be much different now, can it?"

Colly climbed to the pulpit, adjusted robe and script, detailed the perception of the "abatvoix" to ornately direct her words through the abaxial ray of light about her head. "Abba!" she palindromed, raising her arms to the sky, beckoning, maybe begging (she would have enjoyed the abbacy...who wouldn't enjoy the opportunity to abuse power and affect the process of individuation?).

Mofo heard a story from an old Skin Worker concerning the last Abbasside who ruled at Baghdad in 1249 A.D. "We were, how do you say, abbatial ... " he had said while Mofo watched him tighten the skin, "but I wasn't an abbe or an abbess. The last monk was beheaded in front of the abbey for public entertainment. Head in the basket, body on the slab, an Abbey Lubber to be sure. The abbot wept false tears. The crowd jeered and cheered. Who would lay claim to the abbotship next? Who would have the courage? It seemed as if the entire act were nothing more than an "abbozzo," an abbreviated textual version of history as it would continue to happen with nobody to disagree...

The Skin Worker didn't finish the narrative he'd begun, but fell silent and returned to his work. Maybe there was no conclusion, no drawing of briefs, but a reduction of petitions, a return to the chancery in Rome. Abridged History is generally overlooked, but when the antenna snaps, a repairman will be called. It is important that we find out how the show turns out: unfinished history goes unscathed in a senseless riot of lies.

Colly closed the book and breathed a scintillating sigh. Mofo nodded plausibly. The music faded out and lights dimmed. The director called for a five minute break, allowing the actors to pause and contemplate the heaviness of double gravity.

KARYOSHKIN AND (OTHER) FICTIONS A (NOVEL)

"The fire's flames cast a strange red light upon the mud walls, underneath the stars."
(*The Diary Of Isabelle Eberhardt*, EI-Merayer, 30 July 1900)

(While the bombs begin to fall).

Two faces floated in the cloudy orange light of the fire. Winter night, the smell of coming snow in the air, sound of summer crickets in the eyes of one of the faces. Tears: the face wishes it could go back in time, back to the sound of summer crickets. The other face is content and unaware of its companion's sadness. "The world will snow," the sad face said. "Yes," the content one said, "it will be beautiful."

(Laurel And Hardy).

A Definition (From The Italian): Dolce Far Niente: Sweet Do-Nothingness.

(Reminds me of an old girlfriend).

The writer Karyoshkin walked into the concert hall, took a program, and put his bag down to save a seat for himself while he left the hall to go to the bathroom. He walked through the lobby and downstairs to where the restrooms were. He took a piss in one of the stalls, looked quickly at his face in the mirror, ran his hand through his hair, and pushed open the door. His stomach sank, hope disappeared from the world, and little fire horses danced circles around his feet.

Karyoshkin ran up the stairs, walked quickly into the concert hall, picked up his bag, and went out into the night. He was careful to not meet the eyes of strangers who passed on the street. Until his mind stopped racing, the writer Karyoshkin would speak to no one, not even the bookstore owner, who gave Karyoshkin cigarettes and beer and let him sit undisturbed in a comfortable chair with his feet up on his desk.

(All at once fear and desire came into the room).

The bookstore owner stared out at the empty rain-filled street. He lit a cigarette, smoked it, and lit another. He looked out at the street. He looked at his books. He wished someone would come in out of the rain to buy a book, but the streets were empty, except for the rain, which went about its business of wetting everything down. Across the street, a man came out of the bank, opened his umbrella, and walked quickly down the street towards home. The bookstore owner sighed.

(The first moth of the season taps the bulb).

"Everywhere is burning." (Konrad Bayer, "The Bird Sings," 1957-1958)

(At the same time, a strange train passes).

But what are friends for? Space came by plane. Time came by boat. Space crashed, time sank.

(Edna threw a firecracker out the window).

Everything is done by hand. Karyoshkin writes by hand, Karyoshkin types by hand. He bakes bread and cakes, all by hand. He walks allover the city, by hand, he hands his papers to the policeman, by hand, he thinks of running away, hand in hand, but waits until the policeman scratches something into a notebook, by hand.

Karyoshkin wrung his hands together so hard that four tears of tears fell out and broke on the ground. Karyoshkin reached down, picked up the broken pieces and dropped them into a thimble.

(Tired of the escalating violence)?

A Definition (From the German) Sehnsucht: Addiction To Longing.

(An undying faith in love as bad as religion).

"Mr. Blurr said: This is a house that was once a house." -- (Russell Edson, "Mr. & Mrs. Blurr," From *What A Man Can See*).

(First, embers become leaves, then frogs).

The writer Karyoshkin sat on the edge of his bed with his head in his hands (love-jilted Karyoshkin). He raised his head and stared into space for a while, but no thoughts came. He lay down on his bed with his overcoat on top of him as a blanket. He wrapped the overcoat tightly around his body, as if bracing for a cold wind, and folded his hands on his chest. This is what Karyoshkin will look like when he is dead, he thought, but the mortician probably won't allow my dead body's legs to be crossed.

He wished he had remembered to close his window shade. He didn't want the neighbors to be able to see his body if he died and they looked through his window. He wished he had the strength to rise from the bed and pull the shade. Then the phone rang.

The word "hope" flashed as a picture in Karyoshkin's mind, a picture of his beloved's face. He lifted the receiver, but it was not her, it was only his friend, the writer Karpenin.

"I'm cooking a stew," the writer Karpenin said.

"Okay." Karyoshkin said, and hung up the phone. "Perhaps I won't die today after all," he thought, and rose from his bed.

(Dumplings).

THINGS THAT HAPPEN

Whenever I leave my house, I expect something to happen which will change my whole life. I wait for it until I go home again. That is why I never stay in my room. Unfortunately nothing has ever happened.

--Emanuel Bove, *My Friends*

Whenever I am unable to sleep I stare at the ceiling and ask "Is my life interesting? What will happen to me?" I keep a notebook next to my bed to write down some of the things that have happened to me. Most people don't take the time to write things down. They forget their days and think that nothing ever happens to them, but things are always happening. Sometimes we aren't aware of this fact because the things we want to happen to us don't happen, and the things that do happen to us don't seem important enough to think about. As for me, I like to wander and look around. Things always happen when I wander. Nothing happens when I stay at home, so I keep wandering. I believe that if you wait long enough, *everything* will happen.

Wednesday

I went to the supermarket to buy some seedless grapes. I pushed my cart to the produce department, picked a grape from one of the bunches and put it in my mouth. I spit it out and decided to buy a different kind of fruit since I work hard for my money and only like to buy things I know I will like. Later that night, I walked into town to see a film I saw last week. I liked it so much the first time that I wanted to see it again. While I was walking to town I saw the shadows cast by two objects on the ground by the light of a street light. I stood above the objects and studied them. One was a rock. The other object was also round, but smaller than the first. I gently pressed down on it with the toe of my shoe. It was soft but slightly resilient. If I had pressed any harder I would have crushed it, so I stopped pressing, moved my foot, and leaned down to have a look. It was a seedless grape. I lifted it gently to my mouth and placed it on my tongue. Delicious. I walked to town, a little faster than I had been walking before finding the grape.

Thursday

I found a dead fly in the sink and washed it down the drain. My gums bled when I brushed my teeth. In bed, I thought I saw a centipede wriggling on the sheet, but it was a pine needle.

Friday

I had a tooth dream. In my dream, I stood next to the window in a hotel room. Someone from one of the upper floors threw down a television. It struck me in the mouth, knocking out my left front tooth. There was a lot of blood and mucus on my hand. I began to panic when I realized I would need the services of a dentist. In the dream, it occurred to me I was having a dream.

I told myself to wake up, opened my eyes, looked out the window and saw the sky was clear and blue. I was sweating, but my tooth was intact. A woman living in the apartment below mine was playing an acoustic guitar and singing, "the black bird loves you, the black bird loves you."

Saturday

I talked about fever games with a friend today. I told her I would like to write in my notebook about the kind of games the mind makes up and plays when the body is in fever, but I thought it would be nearly impossible since it is hard to recall the rules of these games when health has returned the brain to its normal operating capacity. My friend wished there was a pill you could take to make the brain play fever games when it wasn't sick. I said that if there was such a pill I would surely take one often.

Sunday

I sat on a bench in the park. An old woman sat down next to me. After about ten minutes, she got up and said, "Bye Ned." My name is not Ned.

Monday

I couldn't fall asleep. I kept tossing and turning and swirling ideas in my head. My mind wouldn't stop working. At three in the morning I got up for a glass of water. When I went back to bed, I noticed the room was darker than it was when I got up. The streetlight in front of my apartment building had gone out. I went to the window. The sky was clear and full of stars. The street, without its light, was dark. I had a strange sensation like a strange presence was passing by the building. I thought something bad was about to happen. The streetlight flickered and came back to life.

Tuesday

I stepped on a wishbone left by someone in the hall. It snapped into four segments. I stared at them for a while, but didn't clean them up. I thought it would have been bad luck for me to touch them with my hands.

Wednesday

I had what I am sure was an important dream but lost it when I woke up and began my day.

Thursday

Haircut.

Friday

I was in the mood for Chinese food, so I called the restaurant and placed an order. The man on the phone said my food would be ready in fifteen minutes. I grabbed a jacket and walked out the door. It was too warm for a jacket, so I wrapped it around my waist and tied the sleeves together like a belt. "Charlie!" a woman yelled from her kitchen window. "Hey Charlie!" She walked out into her yard. I didn't see anyone in the street, so I wondered who she was shouting at. "Charlie!" she yelled. I looked over my shoulder and saw she was yelling at me. She opened her gate and approached me on the sidewalk. I kept walking but turned and, walking backwards, shouted, "I'm not Charlie!"

She stopped in mid step, squinted and said, "you're not Charlie."

"No. I'm not," I said. "But you live next door?" she asked, pointing to the house next to hers.

"No," I said, "I don't." I turned and kept walking down the street. I heard her door shut behind me.

My name is Jack.

When I turned the corner, I found two men hunched over a block of ice. They wore green overalls and looked like moving men. One of them held a piece of paper on which there was some kind of diagram while the other chipped away at the block with a small chisel. I heard one of them say, "no, not there, here."

When I returned to that part of the sidewalk with my food, the chipped remnants of the block of ice were melting into little puddles.

Saturday

I walked by a telephone pole today. Its rungs were close enough to the ground so that anyone could climb to the top if they wanted to. I'd like to climb the pole one day, but I'm not sure what I would do after I reached the top.

Sunday

I almost stole a newspaper from the newsstand today, but decided against it at the last minute. I used to be a good thief but that has changed. I'm no longer a good thief because I think too much. A good thief will either think only about the thing he is going to steal and how he is going to steal it or he thinks about nothing and steals automatically. A good thief never thinks about the consequences of his actions while he is in the act of stealing. I always think about the consequences of what I do.

Monday

I worked in the lab this morning. The day had not yet decided if it was going to be hot or cold or wet or dry. Later it rained, but I can't remember now if it was hot or cold. I washed test tubes all morning and thought about getting a second part time job to fill in the afternoons. I might call a woman tomorrow to see if she will let me work in her garden again. I worked for her last year. I thought about my financial situation for a while, but stopped after a few moments had passed. There is nothing more depressing to me than my financial situation.

Tuesday

I walked through town today and noticed the laundry next to the ice cream parlor had a Help Wanted sign taped to the window. I decided almost instantly I didn't want to work there and kept walking. The day decided to rain. My feet got wet, but I tried to not care. Earlier in the day I found an untouched, unread newspaper on the floor of the library's lobby. A day outdoes itself when it gives a free newspaper and makes me feel like something interesting has been coughed up out of the throat of the mundane.

Wednesday

I stared out the window while washing test tubes today. I enjoy the view every morning of the same three trees, the same brick building across the way.

Thursday

On my way home at three in the morning I found a crate filled with artichokes. I didn't take any home. It's all right to stop and ponder a full crate of artichokes at three in the morning, but you'd be a fool to take them home with you. At three in the morning, on an empty, poorly lit street, the only artichoke I'd take home would have to be my own.

Friday

I listened to the ringing bells of a distant church. At four in the morning, only three bells tolled. "Idiot," I said, looking at my clock and thinking about the incompetent bell ringer. As if in response to my remark, the bell tolled once more.

Saturday

It rained today. I ran into a friend in front of the church. We talked about the rain, just long enough for both of us to discover that neither of us thought it was very pleasant to stand there talking in the rain with our feet getting wet. We said goodbye and went our separate ways. I bought a lottery ticket at the newsstand.

Sunday

People continue to mistake me for someone else. A man ran up behind me today, said "Hey Franz..." and stopped smiling when he saw I was not Franz. "Sorry," he said. I shook my head and kept walking. I wondered if anyone else had ever mistaken someone for me.

Monday

I walked home from town today. When I got home I remembered that I had driven into town and parked at a meter. I locked my door, walked to town, and got my car.

Tuesday

I took a short nap today and dreamed about writing in my notebook. Half of what I write I remember writing in dreams I've had weeks, months, or even years earlier. Sometimes when I walk past a mirror I don't recognize myself.

Wednesday

Walking home from town tonight I saw a dead squirrel in the street. I walked toward it and leaned down for a closer look, bracing myself for the sight of spilled internal organs. The moment I expected to be affected by the grotesque ruins of the squirrel, though, it was no longer a dead squirrel but a branch from the tree above. The streetlight's play of shadows on my imagination had modified the branch into its nighttime being.

Thursday

More things happen to me when I am alone than when I am with friends. I notice things more when I am alone. When I am with my friends I like to make them the center of my attentions. Things always happen, but friends come and go.

Friday

A full day today. I wanted to buy a newspaper from a vending machine on the corner in town. It cost thirty-five cents. I found a quarter and a dime in my pocket and read the directions on the machine before dropping them into the slot. The machine said any combination of coins could be used, but not pennies.

I put my coins in the coin slot and pulled the handle to open the door, but the door would not open. I shoved and rattled the machine until a few people looked at me as if I was doing something wrong. I wanted to explain myself to them, but decided against it. I pressed the coin return button on the side of the machine. My dime fell into the slot but my quarter remained somewhere inside. I swore and hit the machine's window with my fist. I turned and walked down the sidewalk, muttering to myself. A woman looked at me with raised eyebrows and an expression of amusement and condescension. She didn't understand my anger.

"It's one thing after another," I thought, walking into the post office. The man behind the counter made a joke about stamps I didn't understand, but I laughed to pretend it had made perfect sense to me. After I laughed, though, it struck me that what he said might not have been a joke after all, since he wasn't smiling or laughing. "Is that all?" he asked, sliding the single stamp I needed across the counter.

Outside, I licked the stamp and put it on my envelope. There were two pennies on the ground, tails up. It would have been bad luck to touch them or pick them up to make wishes, so I left them where they were and walked home.

I heard one man say to another man: "He carves fruit out of wood that looks more real than real fruit."

Saturday

On the way home I saw a stone that had been knocked out of its hole. I leaned down and put the stone back into its hole, feeling as if I had restored a small bit of natural order.

Sunday

I found a beautiful leaf in the street today and carried it home with me. It was half green and half brown like the swirling pattern of military camouflage. Half the leaf was dead, the other half was alive. I carried it in my right hand and thought I would drop it along the way, but as I walked and studied the leaf's intricacies I no longer wanted to let it go. I brought it home and put it on one of my bookshelves. I'll leave it there until it is no longer beautiful.

Monday

I drove to the supermarket today. A soft rain was falling, the roads were wet and shiny, and a grey fog hung low above the ground. I parked and sat in my car listening to the radio, watching the windshield wipers go back and forth.

Tuesday

I was a few minutes late for work today and made up a story to explain my tardiness to my supervisor. I told her that on the way to work I had walked through a parking lot and saw a parked car with an old woman sitting in the driver's seat. Her eyes were closed, she was very old, and I couldn't tell if she was alive or dead. I knocked on the window. She opened her eyes, rolled down the window and asked what I wanted.

"Nothing," I said. "I just wanted to see if you were all right." "I'm fine," she said, rolled up her window, and closed her eyes.

Wednesday

I ate cake in my room tonight while listening to classical music on the radio. A piece of my cake fell onto the floor. I leaned down, picked it up, and put it in my mouth, only to discover I had picked up a small piece of thready fuzz. I spit the fuzz out, found the piece of cake, and threw both of them into the garbage.

Thursday

Today I saw a woman with a nosebleed leaning against a tree. Later, I tripped while crossing the street. I looked back to see what I tripped over, but the street was flat.

Friday

I smiled and said hello to a woman who didn't smile back or say hello to me.

Saturday

I bought a bottle of mineral water today and dropped it on the sidewalk before I had a chance to take a sip from it. A man laughed from behind his window. He must have been standing there all day waiting for me to drop my bottle and make him laugh. I walked home hoping that in the morning, when the man walked outside in bare feet to pick up his newspaper, he would forget about the broken glass. Some strangers don't know how to act.

Monday

I lost my apartment key today and had to climb from the branch of a tree to my open window on the second floor. I ripped my pants, scraped my chin, and found the key in my pocket when I got inside. It was wrapped up in some dollar bills and a receipt. Outside it is raining, but inside I am home for the night.

YELLOW LEATHER

When you approach what you are looking for, the exact center of what you wanted to find, it is because you have worked your way slowly from the outside in. This is the secret of maps and unknown places. You consult the index, you memorize a number, and with a finger of one hand you trace a line from the number while another finger from the other hand traces a line from the letter, until the two meet where you want to be, your destination, the place where the thing is going to happen.

Next, you look to see where this center lies in relation to the surrounding areas. You have never been there before and nothing looks familiar. You trace your path around the center, the place you want to be at a given time for a given event, until you run across a street you know, a main highway from which to navigate, or a solid landmark to fasten onto as you work your way back.

Now you are able to take up pen and paper to write directions to yourself, third left, second right, straight ahead, left at the fork, pass the one-way street, turn left, park, settle in, take a deep breath. You are there, and now you settle in to enjoy the event, the center of attention, your reason for working your way in from the known edges, closer now, closer to the unvisited circle.

Visiting the place for the first time enables you to create a memory, something to store away for the future. You'll be able to say, "Remember?" Maybe the center is only a physical space, a place or thing you want to see, and passing through again is merely due to nostalgia, the urge to remind yourself that you were there then, and · you are there now, and where has all the time gone between? You move on, but the memory has already grabbed hold of you and latched on, you are unable to forget, it is part of you and there is nothing you can do to separate yourself from it, ever.

His mind is now processing images and names and faces and places. There is an important piece missing. The first piece. He thought that any piece would do to begin the puzzle, but he now realizes that two are needed. One piece at the center of the card table is very pretty, but it doesn't tell us much. It doesn't tell us if it is even a part of the puzzle we are trying to put together. For all we know, it is a false piece of cardboard, tossed in carelessly, or with malicious intent to deceive and confuse that bears no relation to the others in the box.

No, one piece is not enough to begin a puzzle. Two pieces lead to a third, and a fourth, and ultimately to the finished picture. What he is trying to grasp is not at the edges of memory, it is part of the middle, part of the root of continuity. They tell him that everyone knows you are supposed to start at the border of the puzzle, then fill in the frame, but it is the frame he has forgotten.

He is trying to wake up and the only way he can wake up is to grasp the middle and pull himself to the edge. He's dreaming. There is something pulling at him, a terror, the emotion that precedes the dream's pictures, the thing that says, "you are going to dream now, brace yourself." He is walking across a room. He has gotten up from the bed and is now walking towards the couch.

"There are the windows," he thinks. The windows are behind the couch now where before there was only a wall. He knows he must open one of the windows to let something in.

A long hairy claw tears the window from its frame and grabs him by the neck. He struggles but quickly gives up. He feels himself fading away. He gives in to it and there is a buzzing in his ears and he thinks, "I have to get out of this dream now."

He bolts upright in bed, searching the room for what sounds like a swarm of insects. The clock radio is on and with the buzzing comes the beating of drums. He relaxes and falls back into his pillow. The buzzing is the vibration of violin strings coming from the radio, strangely manipulated to mimic a swarm of deadly insects.

"Another day," he thinks, studying his hotel room surroundings. The phone rings. Someone says, "good morning, this is your wake up call."

It's all the things he threw away that bother him the most. The pictures, the letters, his irretrievable past. Like the tourist map to the country he will never set foot in again, the pictures were places and reference sources to look at, to see where he had been, where he was going, and where he ended up.

He saw now that he was in a situation, how important those things were and are. He can see the letters, remember some of the words, but most of them, like the faces, have faded away, crumbled like the disintegrating paperbacks he was saving to read on a rainy day, or any other day he might need them for a quick answer, a truth to the day's question.

Like now. Now. And now. And especially now. He has thrown away crucial evidence. History stands corrupted and he can only fill in the pieces, like a tyrant, the way he wants them to be seen. He has in mind now a face, a simple face, a face of magnitude and proportion. He has in mind this one face, now, this simple, evolving face, resembling each number after one, each a total change, a complete difference, but at its core, the One, the single One common to every other One, each number in the progression simply the next One in line, the same, but, as if donning a new mask over the old one for each new day's masquerade, something new and more terrifying each time he looks, each time he sees, each time he realizes this face is not his.

He has the impression that something like this has happened before, not in another life but in the lives of his ancestors, as if in all the family snapshots handed down through the ages there was an empty space waiting to be filled. What form of immortality does the photograph make? It makes an immortality that will last a lifetime, if not lost or thrown away.

A photograph can save some of the irretrievable, it can buoy the sinking boat of forgotten memories and sustain it until the final tidal wave crashes down. A photograph has its own strange and fortuitous existence.

Once brought into the world, the photograph is much like a person, seen or not seen, regarded or ignored, understood or misunderstood, laughed at or admired, remembered or lost to time. To be captured on film is to be captured in a transient universe and passed between finger painting hands, jailed in albums, auctioned off on postcards, circulated worldwide in magazines and newspapers and stuck up on gallery walls.

All those silent pictures scream at you to be seen. Look and memorize, the twofold billfold album, memorize the face that is carried in your wallet of memories. Put them in your back pocket. In a box at home, you keep the negatives, and in your head you keep the memories that surround the photograph, the things beyond the borders. Some you will lose, some you will throw away, some will shrivel and fade. Some will be forgotten, and one day the original will fade and disappear.

There are many ways to observe a photograph. The first of which entails that the observer must keep in mind that he or she is observing an observation. The photograph is past, present and future, it is the fleeting glimpse captured and caged and put on display.

The photograph is silent, but when observing a photograph, there is never an awareness of this silence because the photograph seeps into all the senses, not only the memory. A photograph confuses the senses. In the image, there is no room for silence. When we look at a photograph, the photograph becomes us.

Everything is imagined as it happens. There is never any particular order to anything. There is only the endless string of time and a magic marker staining it at intervals along the way. It is all wound around the package wrapped in brown paper, stamped Fragile or Do Not Crush. Strings are pulled, strings fray, strings snap, and strings burn. Strings also make music.

The future is always as ruined and lost as the present and distant past, strewn behind this future rubble. To be in the future is an eternal task. To *be* the future is impossible. A photograph is the only transportation forward in time, yet even as I arrive on film at the doorstep of my destination I am ruined, flat, flammable, without any sense of the present.

An image is regarded more seriously than a text. Where there are no words there is often a better understanding. A picture never meanders. There is no such thing as a run-on photograph. A moving picture can meander, but a single picture never wanders far from its content. A picture never lies. The point of words, then? To make up and describe pictures. If a picture is worth a thousand words, are a thousand words worth a picture?

One thousand words, three, now five, now seven, so on into the infinities, the point being to depict the worth of a picture without picturing a picture in words, like stacking pennies, five to the nickel, ten to the dime or two nickels, twenty-five to the quarter or two dimes and a nickel, fifty to the half dollar or two quarters or four dimes and two nickels, one hundred to the dollar (bill or coin) or two half dollars or four quarters or...

It comes in waves, all day, every day, everywhere. Cameras click and whir and film, capturing, saving and recording, reproducing, recreating, maintaining a record. If only all of the images filmed in the course of one period of twenty-four hours were to be accumulated and presented on a mosaic of screens against a monumental wall, the one true picture of the world would emerge. So much filming, canning, so much recording, there are two worlds now, or more, the real world, the filmed world, the remembered world (history/memory), and the world of dreams, of or relating to the former. The only way to feel connected is to turn on the television or go to a movie or carry a camera.

What is real? There are no souls left to steal.

—

JAH MUSIC

The stories that are narrated in detective novels can profitably be described as stories of writing and reading insofar as they are concerned with authoring and deciphering "plots."

The plot of the classical detective novel comprises two basically separate stories—the story of the crime (which consists of action) and the story of the investigation (which is concerned with knowledge).

The assumption of, and the search for, a hidden story inscribed in everyday reality has the effect of transforming the world of the novel into a conglomeration of potential signs. All phenomena may lose their usual, automatically ascribed meanings and signify something else.

The lonely and (socially) marginalized intellectual is shown to possess the power to defuse the threats of disrupting social forces by simply reading, that is, interpreting and explaining them.

"The Detective As Reader: Narrativity And Reading Concepts In Detective Fiction." Peter Huhn, Modern Fiction Studies, Volume 33, Number 3, Autumn 1987.

I am constantly going out of my way for total strangers, revealing things before they've uncovered them themselves. I don't like to have surprises ruined by exploding fireworks. The world operates in subtle ways. Patience is the key to discovery. I spend a lot of time lingering in subway stations, watching the full and empty cars pull in and out. I don't know what I am waiting for. Is it narcissistic to want to build a monument before you die? I don't want to be remembered, but I do want to leave behind a legacy, something by which people will remember to not forget. I sit now and wait for tomorrow because tomorrow is the day when it all begins.

I am an avid reader, by which I mean to say that I read a lot and look for deep meaning. So it is with great interest that I study the word ABRACADABRA: formed from the letters of the abraxas, its pronunciation, according to Julius Africanus, was equally efficacious either way. According to Sere nus Sammonicus it was used as a spell to cure asthma.

And ABRAXAS, supreme god of the basilidian sect of Gnostics, of the 2nd Century. Believed his name contained great mysteries, as it was composed of the seven Greek letters which form the number 365. Demonologists have described him as a demon, with the head of a king and with serpents forming his feet. These things I read in John Allegro's *The Sacred Mushroom And The Cross*, 1970. Encyclopedia Of Occultism & Parapsychology, Leslie Shepard, Editor.

I woke up next to a babbling brook. I remember opening my eyes and seeing a white flower petal float by, its head turned the other way, indifferent to my situation. I spent time in a hospital, an institution, a think tank, and a home. Now that I am rehabilitated, certain lights have started flashing in the pinball machine of my mind. I found a photocopy of a letter I sent the previous year. It was the first flake of the so-called avalanche. In it, I described a character who discovers love as an answer to life's many problems. He discovers love and loses it. The book this character appears in will be a deconstructed detective yarn that involves the numerology and semiotics of its characters. It will be written using a pyramid structure, but also the geography of Los Angeles.

I wrote in the notebook that everybody was asking "why?" I was getting tired of the question. Everybody was looking for something else, a second thing, a substitute, an alternative. They had discovered one thing and now sought another before fully exploring the first. They had allowed themselves to become bored. "A secret name is a way of escaping the world," Don Delillo wrote. Moby Dick = Mocha Dick = Richard Mocha. See? Or Melmoth: The name of a man who sells his soul for eternal life in *Melmoth The Wanderer*, famous novel of terror and mystery by Charles Maturnin. Oscar Wilde's pseudonym after prison was: Sebastian Melmoth. Then there's a page of definitions: *Detective (Noun)* A person, often a policeman, whose work is investigating and trying to solve crimes, watching suspected persons, getting information, etc. *Detective (Adjective)* Fitted for detecting, employed in detecting, of or for detection. *Detenebrate:* To remove darkness from. Then this diagram:

1. ABRACADABRA-
2. ABRACADABR-
3. ABRACADAB-
4. ABRACADA-
5. ABRACAD-
6. ABRACA-
7. ABRAC-
8. ABRA-
9. ABR-
10. AB-
11. A-

What is before the beginning of a story, and what is after? I imagined the same blank infinity that must be at the end of the universe and that must have existed before The Big Bang, so I had come full circle, I had discovered nothing. The screen was silent, though loud with infinite possibilities, none of which revealed themselves to me. Having come full circle, I had reached both an ending and a new beginning. But is a circle the same thing as a zero? Does the space in the middle of the donut's ring represent emptiness or a donut hole, which we can snap up by the dozen?

There will be a death. We are moving towards it just as it is moving towards us. Imagine a mirror. Now walk towards the mirror until your nose touches your reflection's nose. This is the best illustration of the movement described. In death, we collide with our reflection and pass into our reflection's world just as it passes into ours. There is a fleeting moment of understanding, then darkness, then nothing.

Blaze Fever. B.F. He had been B.D. before, then B.E. He was methodically working his way through the alphabet, exploring all the twenty-six variations of his original, unlettered soul.

"I'm fighting against my own deconstruction," he said. "I'm being manipulated, made to lie. I am not respected as a detective because there is no mystery to solve. It is all so obvious, but I am still driven to the edge."

Had I come too late? Did I miss the show? Or was I too early, the first to arrive? I took my time selecting a seat before I sat down. I neither expected to wait long nor for something to happen soon. I stared at the blank screen, but instead of seeing nothing, I began to invent the show. The lights dimmed and images appeared. Who was I going to speak to first? There were infinite possibilities. I could talk to everyone, find out what they knew and hope to get lucky, hope to piece things together from the voices of a million bystanders who had ideas but not the right ideas. Or, I could talk to the few people who seemed to matter, those who were finite, nearby, accessible.

"What crime?" he asked.

"There has been no crime," I told him.

I climbed to the top of the stairs and looked into Blaze Fever's eyes. I spoke slowly because I wanted to hear how the words sounded out loud. I knew how they sounded inside my head and I knew that they would sound better as they pushed through the air towards Blaze Fever's realm of understanding. I pointed my gun at Blaze Fever's heart and spoke.

"Blaze Fever?"

He nodded, his eyes unafraid but curious.

"I'm flying the airplane now. Shecky put out the lights."

Blaze Fever knew this was the end. He was prepared. With a slight movement of his shoe, he triggered a switch and fell through a trap door in the floor. He fell into darkness towards the bottom of whatever he had been on top of for so long. I put the gun in my coat pocket and walked down the stairs to the bottom of the pyramid. I looked into the faces of the ones who were gathered there to see the end of the spectacle.

"Anyone got a cigarette?" I asked. Someone handed me one. I lit it and inhaled deeply, letting the smoke out slow. It was only a game, but it was my game now. In winning, I had reached a new beginning, a new frontier. Everyone gathered around me and looked into my eyes. I began making up the new rules. The game was life. You couldn't lose.

Does it really matter who tells the story? Is it the I or am I the it? Are you the we or is she them? The matter should be closed before the book is opened because the plot, at least, should be laid out like points on a map. One should be able to follow the course of the story to its logical or illogical end, like a path to the waterfall. There should also be an awareness of the fact that the story has never really "begun," that it simply won't "end;" that there are no physical points in the material world of the book that are actual borders; that characters do not die when the last page has been read, they simply move on like the faces we see waiting on the other side of the tracks for the train to take them in the opposite direction. They disappear, but they do not dissolve. They move into another plane of existence. The story never really begins or ends, but we ease into it, join it somewhere, meet it, hopefully at the right time and the right place, because there is no way that we can fill in the missing pieces unless we have an idea of what the picture on the puzzle box looks like.

I hear footsteps coming this way. My life goes on as you read, but now you aren't listening to me, you are listening to Max Demon. I'll be in the kitchen if you need me. How will it begin and what form will it take? Episodic or linear narrative? What is the time frame? What are its questions and answers? Unconsciousness. Awareness. What comes after enlightened awareness?

The Santa Ana winds were blowing. It was too hot to sleep. I tossed and turned, threw the sheet off the bed. It was damp with sweat. I pointed the fan at my face but still couldn't sleep. I looked at the clock: 2:38 a.m. It was ninety degrees. I got up and stood next to the window, listening to the Santa Anas blowing through the palm trees, watching the leaves shake and tremble as the air moved around them. There weren't many lights on in any of the windows across the street, but people were awake, tossing and turning like I was, waiting for the heat to break or morning to arrive so they could get up and go to work. It felt like morning would come and go a thousand times before it got any cooler. The grey-blue glow of late night televisions flickered in some of the windows, but television wouldn't cut the heat. I threw myself down on the warm bed, turned on the radio and tuned it to the left, where the late night radio was the best.

I lit a cigarette, playing with the music in my head, watching the smoke rise to the ceiling, thinking, "yeah, what's going on here?" The phone rang. My woman never called me that late, so it was going to be a case. I let the phone ring a few times to see how bad they wanted it. It kept ringing and ringing. They wanted it bad. I thought about the rent, the electric, and picked up the receiver.

"Let's assume that I represent an interested party, shall we?" The voice on the other side of the telephone said.

"I'm interested," I said. "Where should I begin?"

"You're a man of reason," The voice said. "Begin at the beginning."

They hung up. The room came back into focus. I lit another cigarette and watched the smoke rise. Reggae played on the radio.

A man of reason knows that pain is only in the eye of the beholder. The guy with a knife doesn't feel a thing. The Voice would feel no pain, but I would, if it came to that. I turned off the radio, got up and got dressed. The night no longer existed for me. I was a man of reason. I looked out my window, down my street. Someone had sprayed a big arrow on the sidewalk. I left the building and walked in the direction the arrow was pointing. Where would I begin? I began at the beginning. I tapped my source on the shoulder. I stood on the bottom rung of the ladder and looked up at the moon. I had a head start on the world. The beginning was at street level and that's where I began.

I walked and walked and walked. The places I was going to visit were not close. The city was huge. Even with a car, you could still drive forever and never arrive. Walking was only slightly different. You had time to see where you were going, even if it was somewhere infinitely in front of you. You had time to assimilate; you remembered where you had been. I'd take walking over driving any day. Maybe I was old fashioned. I knew I was broke.

"Let the good times roll," I thought, and walked on, smoking cigarettes, kicking pebbles that got in my way. My side of the world began to get light. The morning, though, would not bring any change in the weather. It was going to be hotter than the night before and I was going to be in the thick of it. No coastal breezes would save me. The world was waking up. I walked for an hour, then two, and was beginning the third when I came upon my first stop. Harry Dean's. I needed a gun. Harry Dean would get me one. I needed to talk to Kid Ross too. Harry Dean would tell me where to find him, where he was hiding out, absorbed in his paranoia.

"How ya been, Harry?"

"I've been," he said, and handed me a gun wrapped in yesterday's newspaper along with a napkin with Kid Ross's address written on it in pencil. Harry Dean didn't say another word. I turned and walked through the door, up the stairs, back to street level. I had reached the beginning and now stood at the edge of the middle, where everything was going to happen, where everything was going to be written.

I walked on in the direction of Kid Ross's place. I hadn't yet changed direction, but was still making my way towards the mountains on the horizon, as if Blaze Fever stood waiting at the end of a long line paralleling the ocean, as if the voice and Blaze Fever constituted the two points necessary for the formation of a line, as if I was being pulled along a magnetic strip in the ground that only my feet detected. I wished that my search was really that simple, but something told me that the shape of my movement, if charted out on a map, would prove to be more complicated than a simple straight line. I had the vague sense that I understood what was happening to me, but that this understanding existed a few minutes into my future. As if someone, an alternative version of me, was running just ahead and taking it all in.

There was nothing to do but wait.

A SMALL HERD OF TAME LADDERS

Rubber balls and broomsticks, lightships and jelly cones, top hats and ambiance, aluminum cans and cowhide, trickling thunder and snowflakes, master keys and understatement, translucence and windsocks, dam building and tree felling, caged rabbits and postage stamps, typed drawings and synapses, new tricks and old hats, ear muffs and nose guards, love relics and urban souvenirs, rib tackle and blister bait, straight face and black eye, subtle disguise and silent screams, stripped tubes and hot oils, apple blood and lingerie fur, leaning trees and singing women, clay jugs and green glass, boxer shorts and lion tamers, test patterns and bullet Vaseline, Jell-O archaeology and lemonade hubcaps, laugh tracks and confined wisdom, left marks and wrong turns, exchange rates and dime games, long lines and pock marks, thick windows and liar lions, ink spots and chuckle snails, trail turns and railroad rind, pasted feathers and yellow corn, spotted signs and wire herds, Jell-O juice and fetid fog, green bagels and antler toothpaste, foam shrouded tong and tossed worm, spectral illumination and astral rejection, psychokinetic jury duty and pasted transformations, snug fit and mug warmth, scissor sit and hoof print tint, a soiled saucer in the sink, a glass-eyed captain led to drink, a coddled clam that has no vice, a leather lamb behind thrown rice, hard luck larks and cotton sharks, terry cloth towels and hanging regrets, the presence of substance in thought, ah, the sleep of thirst.

Acquired tastes run through the family, raisins as individual as snowflakes, warmed ice is cold water, lottery tickets and spent winnings, gramophone ear spinning and loom-woven sadness, steam buns and broken buttons, knowing smirks and hood winks, gun pasting takes much longer than the cutting, long legs and ankle craters, clam dip and apple sauce, lingering guests and private tablecloths, pools of bottled water and wax drippings drying, white whispers and quiet shadows, digestive tracts and dead end streets, paging devices and jagged heel stones, salad ice and powder straws, green buds and white lace, torn baggies and ashtray sponges, burning tables and sink mirrors, open windows and gutter sensations, angry typists and insomnia smoke, sharpened pencils and melted red wax, open eyes and thought-provoking stares, an unglued mess, chained madness, basketball dribble, pillows of numbness, the host's car pulling away from the curb, what's the name of that song they sing in French when nothing matters anymore?

The fact that is forgotten in a cloud of fancy evasion sparks no concern. Silence is louder than song, the easily satisfied give up before the find. We are masters of disguise.

Riot guns and acid houses, parking violation and timeout call, ambulance crashes and taxi crowds. Milk, water, juice, and bread, these are fine times for thin cigars, these are blind times for broken stars. Valley sheaf and syllable claws hoof and nose, flank and pose, wounded forge and coupled string, taking walks and eroding things. We watch and wonder, but no tender opens the door, no man breaches the code of conduct, no woman recreates her role for the stage.

Shadow dancing and button pushing, island clearing and wall hangings, rusty paint and chipped metal, a hen, a trick, a razor blade, a muscle tear, an aching back, a fox, a coarse hour, a cufflink.

Inside the outside wail, up above, down beyond. Wait. Make it worth the while. To color a human response, to link the missing round, the way, the road, the house, your bed: each day brings it closer.

A ribbon-lined remark, a gift in your mouth, a voice of reason, pieces of love coursing through the popular vein, of course, yes, of course. Before the fact, a hurdle to cross, a new sphere to circle and punch, a death to kill or wait for, people you've yet to meet and know, walking barefoot through lava... In limbo it is always time to eat.

223

Tight dry skin in the drawer, a red book in the key, a lamp the promise of warmth. Little things gathered into pools of significance, laughter down the hall. Behind closed doors, private scenes. The porch, the unused television, words, faces, and eyes, what to do, what to do?

Tobacco and marmalade, yellow sponges and nickel lies, soft skin and pale beginnings, lost in shadow, shadowed in doubt, an endless beginning, a page out of fear, another one left to rot by the side of the road, oily head and locust swarm, dirt clog and tree pulp, cod lamb and road rig, a day is no good without a stroll through the park.

Bishop shears and foal fodder, baked bread and donut holes, long shores and rough signs, where were you when the shooting began? Head west to her, head west to the edge, the ocean lip of understanding, May Day, the capsule's breaking up, watch for yellow fish, unconnected dots, are you along for the journey or just for the ride?

Rounding up the herd, polishing the silver, erasing old debts, settling claims, discovering truths, clearing the debris, be patient, please, if only that, you're an opiate, remember and forget. Meet me in the middle, are you game? Meet me there, meet me anywhere, crawl, ooze from sleep into waking dream.

What a terrible film, I wish you'd been there. Hours pass, days run, the earth spins your marking pin. String, wire, words, methods of salutation, objects of connection, shared peaks and valleys. When our ball finally drops, will it bounce or break? The answers are sealed inside white envelopes. Head west to who? You? You're standing there. Me? I've run out of lines.

SEVEN: PERMEKE'S CONSTANT

(Book One: The Three Graces)

ONE

Gladly fell to the ground. Blood poured from the top of his head and down his face. He blinked and wiped his eyes with a shaking dirty hand. In the flash of a bomb burst on the side of the hill above him he saw the pool of his own blood as it formed in the dust beneath his face. Rock and clods of dirt fell from the sky, hitting him in the back. He poked a finger into his blood and felt its warmth. Another round of explosions came after a second of silence. The ground shook beneath him. Several times he was bounced towards the night sky.

He did not want to touch the place on his head where he was bleeding. They had been told stories about men who, in shock after having a portion of their skulls blown off, stuck their fingers or hands into their heads and pulled out pieces of their brains. They had been told that these men did this while running through the trenches, or seated on a rock in the middle of the battlefield, legs crossed as if they had stopped on a walk through the country to enjoy the scenery. Gladly knew he was going to die. He wanted it to happen quickly.

His helmet was nowhere in sight. The ground heaved beneath him and flipped him onto his back. Someone shot up a flare. He opened his eyes and found himself on the beneath a gray leafless tree. Someone's body was wedged between two branches and hung, half-stuck, half-dangling, as blood poured from his neck where the head had been just minutes earlier.

The flare landed somewhere on the battlefield and went out. He stood up and ran. None of the soldiers he ran past heard or saw him. They were all in shock, dead, dying, or screaming themselves. Gladly ran into the night, his hands reaching forward as if he were running to hug someone he had not seen in a long time.

He ran until dawn. The sky was gray with the first hint of day. He was somewhere near the town where they had been posted the night before. He had run four miles into what

226

was now enemy-held territory. There was nothing left of the town but a few pock-marked walls here and there standing precariously next to piles of brick, wood and glass. Some chickens squawked and pecked among the ashes. Thick black smoke rose from the chimney of the schoolhouse, the only building left standing. Thick black smoke rose from the chimney. Gladly pushed the door open and looked inside. An old woman shoved papers into the cast-iron stove where he had warmed himself the night before. A soldier stood behind her with a gun raised to her head. When he saw Gladly framed in the doorway with the pale blue-grey of dawn behind him like a theater backdrop, the soldier put the pistol to his head and pulled the trigger.

The old woman didn't flinch. She acted as if she had not noticed what happened, or as if she did not care. She continued to push papers into the flames with a stick she also used as her cane. She was shoving maps into the flames. Gladly stepped into the room, walked up to the old woman, and touched her shoulder. She did not turn around to look at him. She did not speak. Gladly could not see what she looked like. Her features were covered with blood and black soot. She hummed to herself and continued to put maps in the fire.

"Where am I?" Gladly asked.

He didn't know if the old woman could understand him. He didn't know if he was really speaking or if his mouth was just moving in a pantomime of sound, a hallucination of words. He looked down at the soldier who had shot himself in the head. He was an officer. Gladly turned to leave. The old woman clicked her tongue. She looked straight at him now, raised her cane and pointed to a framed picture on the wall.

A red horse the color of dried blood trotted slowly across a field of gently rolling green hills. The sky was filled with billowy white clouds but all the colors in the painting were faded as if it had been hanging on the schoolroom wall for a very long time. When Gladly turned away from the painting, the old woman was gone. A bomb exploded in the distance. He looked out the window. A huge fireball filled the sky. He heard a noise behind him and spun around to see what it was.

The red horse stood watching Gladly, waiting for him to climb on its back. Gladly took a deep breath, grabbed hold of the horse's mane and pulled himself up. The horse whinnied and trotted Gladly across a field, up and then down a hill into a shallow valley, then up another hill to the other side. From the top Gladly could see a village a few miles away. The horse began to gallop. Gladly pressed his legs into the horse's side and leaned forward to avoid being thrown from the saddle.

The sun disappeared behind the eclipsed moon. The sky was filled with a reddish-orange glow as if the whole world was on fire and was throwing flames up into the sky. Gladly heard more thunder in the distance. A shell whistled high over his head and plummeted into the outskirts of the town. The horse slowed to a stop. Gladly dismounted and stood by its side. He listened to a long silence that was finally punctuated with a huge explosion. Again, the ground shook beneath Gladly's feet.

He took a few steps forward, stopped, looked down, and realized that he was not wearing shoes. He did not know where he had lost them. His feet were dirty and bloodied, but he felt no pain. The blood-red horse nudged Gladly from behind with its snout. He stumbled forward and began to walk towards the town. When he had gone a few steps he turned to look behind him. The horse galloped up the hill they had just come down and disappeared behind the other side. Gladly found himself on a path that led through a thicket of trees. The path soon turned into a road that wound through pastures bordered by low stone walls. The dirt beneath his feet was soft and cool. Every step he took kicked up a small cloud of dust. The bomb had fallen into the town cemetery. Gladly walked up to the cemetery's low stone wall to survey the damage. The earth was ripped open by the blast. Tombstones stood around the crater like people staring down into a hole. A dozen coffins had been blown from their resting places. One of them was on fire.

Gladly climbed over the wall and looked down into the hole. A skeleton's hand was thrust through a crack in the side of what remained of the blasted wood casket. Gladly listened to the bones pop as they were consumed by the heat of the flames until a gravedigger came running from the village and startled Gladly.

The gravedigger had seen smoke rising from his cemetery and knew that he might find his grounds torn up, tombstones cracked or shattered into bits, bodies strewn across the grass or blown into pieces. When he saw Gladly standing next to the crater left by the explosion, it looked to the gravedigger as if one of the dead had climbed up from the hole and was now wondering what to do next. When he saw Gladly's torn clothes, his bare feet, his blood-encrusted head, and the dazed look in his eyes, he was sure that one of the fresh graves had been hit and that this man standing in front of him was one of the poor souls who had been buried the day before.

The soot-filled sky cast a pall over Gladly's face. He turned to find the gravedigger looking at him from behind a gravestone twenty feet away. The man's face was filled with a mixture of confusion and fear. Gladly smiled. The gravedigger smiled back and waved. Gladly told himself that if he walked in the direction of the hills over which the red horse had carried him on its back, he would eventually be able to find the schoolhouse and return to the other side of the canvas, but when he took a step in that direction, his chest contracted in pain like a fist had stuck inside his lungs, pressing against his heart with the point of a rusty nail. He could not breathe. He faced the gravedigger and tried to move his lips, but no sound came out. He pointed towards the hill behind which the red horse had disappeared.

The gravedigger nodded and smiled but then shook his head and looked very serious when he pointed towards the road and motioned that Gladly should walk in that direction. Gladly walked slowly away from the crater and climbed over the low stone wall. He put his hands in his pockets, lowered his head, and returned to the dirt road. The pain in his chest eased and he could breathe again. The gravedigger watched Gladly until he disappeared around a bend in the road. He began stamping out flames and wondered what he should do first to restore his cemetery to its original state.

He stood with the tip of the shovel pressed into the ground and looked at the destruction around him. His face was long with sorrow. Even his moustache seemed to have collapsed beneath the strain of the war. He stood without moving for a very long time, until his breathing slowed, his mind stopped thinking thoughts, and he became, for a moment, a statue staring into the distance with a hazy look of sad knowledge in his eyes.

TWO

When Gladly arrived in the town, there were people everywhere moving about the streets, carrying bundles of possessions, clothes, and food on their backs and on carts they pulled or pushed. There were soldiers from both sides in the crowd, but none of them paid any attention to each other.

The sky was dark and red. The church bell was ringing endlessly as if an alarm had been sounded. It appeared to Gladly that everyone in the crowd understood the meaning of the alarm but him. Gladly did not understand their language. Some screamed, some cried, some pulled at their hair as they walked. Others covered their eyes or ears with their hands.

Gladly saw a naked woman lying on the ground in front of the burnt-out shell of a house. Her arms and hands were folded like a pillow under her face. Her skin was gray like stone. She looked like she had been sculpted from the ground and left for all to see. A soldier stepped from the passing crowd and covered the woman with a blanket.

Gladly saw her feet move. She rubbed the heel of one foot against the ankle of the other foot. She looked like she was in shock. A wave of sadness washed over Gladly as he looked at her. He turned away and joined the advancing crowd.

No one seemed to notice that his head was covered with blood, that his uniform was torn to pieces and hanging at his side, and that his feet were bare and dirty. He found a fountain next to a building that looked like it might once have been a hotel or a restaurant before it was bombed and abandoned. He tore off a piece of his shirt, soaked it in the cold water trickling from a small hole in the shapeless mass of stone and washed the blood and dirt from his head and face. He found a piece of hard candy in his pocket and though he could not tell what flavor it was, he rolled it from cheek to cheek on his tongue until the taste of blood was gone.

A man brushed past him, turned and looked over his shoulder. He was tall with an oddly-shaped head and ears so red and swollen they appeared as if they were about to burst. All he carried with him was a cane and a burlap sack slung across his shoulder. He looked at Gladly's feet, pulled a pair of brown leather shoes from his bag, and motioned that he wanted Gladly to try them on.

Gladly looked into the man's eyes. They were two or three times the size of normal eyes and drooped as if weighed down by strings with lead weights. The man's eyes told Gladly nothing about what he was thinking. They looked as if they had been painted onto his face. His arms were long and hung down to his knees. Gladly sat down at the man's feet and tried on the leather shoes. They were a little small but fit him well enough to get him over rock and glass without getting cut or dirty. He stood up and patted the man on the shoulder. "Thank you," he said. The man nodded and said, "These shoes belonged to a teacher who was killed today. You must leave this place with everyone else. You must leave tonight." He turned and walked away.

Gladly followed the man at a distance until he disappeared into the crowd. He smelled coffee, cinnamon, and hashish wafting out of the darkness of a door that led into some kind of den. A man walked out of the shadows inside and melted into the crowd. Gladly stepped through the opening and the door closed behind him. It was too dark to see anything clearly but he could make out the shadows and shapes of figures seated around tables on which dim candles flickered. He saw the orange glow of cigarettes and pipes as they burned in the hazy darkness. He could not see whole faces, just parts of faces as they moved in and out of the shadows. He could not hear anyone speaking, but a low whisper filled the room and rubbed gently against his ears like a ghost trying to be heard.

A woman took him by the hand. She led him to a room at the back of the den. A pile of newspapers sat on the floor against the wall. She sat him down in a comfortable soft chair of plush red velvet and whispered something in his ear that he heard but did not understand. She sat in his lap and ran her hands through his hair. When she touched his face he realized that it was the first time he had been touched since he had been sent to the front months ago. She cupped his cheeks in the palms of her hands and looked into his eyes.

"You're going to be half blind," she said. When he opened his mouth to speak she put her finger to his lips. She put her arms around his neck and pulled his head against her shoulder. At that moment he felt suddenly tired, as if the exhaustion of the past months had finally caught up with him. He closed his eyes and dozed off to sleep for a few minutes. All the time she ran her hands through his hair and whispered things he did not understand.

When he opened his eyes he felt rested. Only a few minutes had passed but he felt as if he had woken up from his first good night's sleep in years. She slid off his lap and went to a wood-burning stove in the corner of the room, where she made a cup of hot tea for him to drink. It was the color of watered-down milk and tasted of cinnamon, honey, nutmeg, and clover. At first the tea made him feel hot and sleepy, but as its warmth spread through his body he began to feel rejuvenated, content, and awake. He drank and watched as she worked near the stove crushing spices in a pestle, mixing them together in a white ceramic bowl.

Only now could he really see what she looked like, how she had some of the same characteristics as the man who had given him the shoes. Her face was swollen in places, making her look like she was both grimacing in pain and smiling at the same time. She wore a loose cloth dress that was brown like cinnamon and red like the horse that had taken him to the town…red like dried blood. He saw blood everywhere as if his eyes had been covered with lenses of blood through which he could only see blood and death and deformity.

He shook his head. His vision cleared and he saw how beautiful she was behind her strange appearance. She had finished working at the table and was on her hands and knees as if she was going to clean the floor, but only rocked back and forth with her eyes closed, humming quietly to herself. There was no pattern to the humming but the sounds lulled him and made him feel calm. When he closed his eyes he saw the red horse with a black bird on its back.

"They are the black birds of happiness," a voice said. Gladly opened his eyes. Did she say that? Her eyes and mouth were closed. She rocked back and forth on her hands and knees. He looked around the small room. He didn't know where he was or what he was supposed to do.

She stood up and disappeared behind the curtain leading back into the main room through which he had walked when he first entered the den. He got up from his chair and followed her but in the darkness he could not tell which shadow was hers. The door swung open and light shot into the room. For a moment he saw all their faces, all of them deformed in some way. Their eyes were filled with sadness. The woman had disappeared. The faces that stared back at him were pale and lifeless. He ran towards the door as it began to swing shut and bolted into the street.

The sky was bright orange. He ran, gasped for breath, and slowed to a walk. He was in the crowd again and looked into the faces of those who were walking in the opposite direction. He looked into their eyes and tried to feel what they were thinking. Everyone seemed to be avoiding everyone else's gaze in their haste to get wherever it was they were going. He lowered his head and walked with the crowd until he found himself at the train station.

People were pushing and shoving each other, jockeying for position as they tried to board the already overcrowded train. Somehow Gladly was able to push through to the edge of the platform. He stepped up onto the train, stood by a window, and looked out at the faces of those who had not been able to climb aboard. Soon the train was up to speed and he was hurtling through the countryside. It was better than running, he thought. He just had to stand on the train and it would take him away.

An hour later, the train pulled into another town. He looked through the window and saw three women sitting next to each other on a bench. They were shrouded in a gray haze, but illuminated as if by a light passing through a crystal. Gladly reached up and wiped the window with his sleeve, thinking that it might be dirty and that he was imagining the haze around their heads, but when he saw that the three women were really sitting inside something that looked like a smoky lens, he stepped off the train and walked towards them. The train's whistle sounded.

Gladly watched as it steamed down the tracks. He looked into each window of every compartment. No one looked out. It was as if they had no interest in seeing where they were going. Gladly saw his face for an instant in the final car's last window. This is a memory, he thought.

"This is a memory," a woman's voice said. Gladly spun around to see who had spoken, but each of the three women appeared to be preoccupied with their own thoughts. None of them seemed to be aware of his presence, though he stood only ten feet away from them. The gray haze enveloped them like the haze he had seen in the daguerreotypes in his family's albums before the war.

Gladly cleared his throat. "Excuse me," he said. They gave no response and made no motion to indicate that they had heard him speak. "Excuse me," he said again, but again there was no response. He sighed and looked down the tracks. A rabbit emerged from some brush, hopped across the rails, and disappeared into the bushes on the other side. Gladly turned his head and looked down the tracks in the other direction. A couple of birds picked at the railroad gravel, searching for seeds or fallen berries.

"It's a memory," Gladly thought again, and again a woman's voice echoed his own and said, "it's a memory."

He stepped into their circle and, once inside, was not able to see the platform or the tracks or anything that had been there for him to see just a second earlier. Inside their hazy sphere they were no longer out of focus, but almost too sharply in focus. They appeared unreal like the deaths he had witnessed on the battlefield.

Just as Gladly knew what was going to happen before it happened, he knew their names were Rachel, Laura, and Elizabeth, and that they were going to take him somewhere.

Sometimes Gladly was able to see the world around him clearly as if for the first time, but also as if he had been alive as long as the universe, so that while everything appeared to be razor-new, there was also the thought that this was how things were supposed to be.

At times like this his breathing slowed and he saw everything as if preserved in a frozen space of time or a captured time of space, the way a clock behind glass slows and for a moment stops before picking up its rhythm again, the way a cobblestone street looks at dawn, just before the sun is up high enough to light one's way, when the lamps still burn but are not needed to see, before the lamplighter has arrived to reach up with his pole and extinguish the flame, the way an orange, thrown into the sky, pauses for a moment at the apex of its trajectory before falling and slapping back into the palm of the hand that launched it.

Just as unexpectedly as these moments of clear sight started, they faded like a lantern light turned down low, or a door swung slowly shut, and Gladly felt as if he had risen to a great height from where he could see everything and, having caught a glimpse of it, was brought slowly back down to the ground where he continued on his way or arrived where he was going, where there was really no way for him to explain what he had seen because the moment he began to understand anything was also the moment he felt like he understood nothing. Rachel's eyes glowed ruby red, Laura's were emerald green, and Elizabeth's were sapphire blue. Rachel closed her book and slipped it into her coat pocket. She stepped forward, touched Gladly's cheek and told him to close his eyes.

"Now open them," she said. Gladly found himself standing next to her near a pool of water. Lily pads floated on the surface. Dragonflies sunned their wings. Rachel led Gladly by the hand in the direction of a palace in the distance. Orange carp and green frogs swam in the water, right up to the base of the palace, where its white dome shined like sun striking snow on a bright day.

Rachel's eyes blinded him whenever he looked at her. If he timed his glances properly, he was able to look at her from the side while her eyes were wandering away from his towards the gardens or the palace in the distance.

As they walked, Gladly could see that Rachel's lips moved, but he could not understand a word she was saying because every time she opened her mouth he heard the fury of a beehive rise from her throat. They walked for what seemed like an hour, and though Gladly did not understand a word of what she was lecturing him about with her beehive voice, understood she was trying to tell him something he needed to know. As they walked hand in hand, a dwarf in a circus master's suit appeared from behind a bush. He stood on the back of a swan that he guided with a pair of reins connected to a ring around its neck and held a silver sphere above his head that, when Gladly looked into its reflective surface, made it look as if they were walking on a small round earth that rolled beneath their feet while the sky rolled in the opposite direction.

Rachel abruptly closed her mouth. The sudden absence of the sound of the beehive startled Gladly. She had led them to a round of grass in the middle of which was a bed made up with white linens. Seven torches burned at the ends of posts stuck in the ground in a circle around the bed. Their flames were invisible in the bright sunlight, but Gladly knew they were lit because heat waves shimmered in the air above the bed, making the palace's white dome look like a mirage dancing above the horizon. The dwarf waved to them and continued on his way.

Rachel led Gladly to a chair outside the circle of torches. She kissed him on the forehead and lifted his chin to make him look into her eyes. Their ruby red glow no longer blinded him. He stared into their flames and felt himself hypnotized into a state of euphoric well-being. In his mind he pictured a winged clock with no hands and no numbers on its face. It danced in a circle around a hole in the earth from which an orange light glowed, as if the hole were filled with pulsating embers or lava.

The winged clock flew towards Gladly like a hummingbird. It buzzed past his head a few times and said, in a voice of alarm clock bells, "There is no time, there is no time," and buzzed off into the trees. Gladly laughed out loud. He didn't know what it meant but thought it was funny.

Rachel walked through the ring of torches, lay down on the bed's white sheets, closed her eyes, and folded her arms across her chest. Her skin in the sunlight looked like the alabaster of a figure Gladly had seen lying supine in a cathedral after it was bombed in the early days of the last offensive. It had been his job to supervise the movement of relics and icons from the church so that the advancing enemy soldiers couldn't get their hands on them. He and a crew of other soldiers had taken the alabaster figure from the lid of its sarcophagus, wrapped it in cloth, and buried it in the ground near a farmhouse not far from the church.

Gladly felt as if they had attended the funeral of a friend. He ordered the other men to return to the camp. When they were out of sight, he picked a bunch of wild flowers and placed them on top of the temporary grave. He marked the spot on a map, smoothed out the dirt with a hoe, and returned to his tent where, for the rest of the day and night, the men spoke only in whispers.

Rachel's body began to vibrate and shake as if she were having a convulsion. Gladly leaned forward in his seat. He didn't know what to do. The buzz of bees filled the air. Rachel melted into a gray fog. He squinted his eyes and tried to see her face, but she was no longer solid and had turned into a writhing mass of bees. They oozed over the edge of the bed to the ground, where they formed a puddle that grew towards the sky into a pillar the shape of Rachel with two magnesium white flares for eyes. The Rachel of bees stepped forward, knocked the seven torches down with a single sweep of her arm and stepped towards Gladly on legs of bees.

The bees swarmed all around him. They wrapped their arms around him and lifted him into the air, and when he felt his feet touch the ground he looked down into the hole around which the winged gold clock had danced. He dove into the hot lava and swam until he could no longer hold his breath and had to come up for air. He found himself near the shore of a lake lined with tall pine trees. Laura sat near the edge of the shore waiting for him, her eyes glowing emerald green. She handed him a towel. Gladly dried himself off and sat down in the sand. She put her arm around his shoulder and spoke softly into his ear.

A fish jumped up out of the water and fell back into the lake with a splash.

238

THREE

They walked away from the lake down a path through woods thick with new snow. Laura held his hand and dictated their movements through the forest. She told him about the people and creatures that populated that part of the country and told him that, although he could not see them, they were everywhere, in the trees, underground, and in the air. Gladly thought he caught glimpses of motion out of the corners of his eyes when she told him this fact, but each time he turned his head he saw nothing but a trembling branch or a puff of snow shimmering in the sunlight as it caught the rays of the sun from the strange sky above. The clouds seemed to move faster here than through the skies of other countries Gladly had visited.

They walked for several hours. The day gave way to night as she led him to the house of one of the forest people tucked away in the corner of a cave of trees. Curtains were drawn shut across every window and shadows moved behind them. The front door opened. Gladly and Laura stepped inside. He expected to be bathed in light, but when he walked into the house it was too dark for him to see his feet. The house was filled with people, but all he could see were their faces, as if they were lit from under their skin. Gladly had expected to be a stranger since he did not recognize the house from the outside, but many of the guests said hello to him or nodded their heads and smiled. He felt like he knew them but could not remember from where or when.

Laura led him through the party. Deep bass rhythms and high tonal shrieks pulsed through his body, but Gladly could not see where the music came from. He could not see a band in any of the rooms, but wherever he looked, people danced as if in a trance. Gladly stopped to watch one of the dancers spin, convulse, and roll her eyes toward the ceiling. All around her, men and women were lost in their own trances, but each of them reached out now and then to touch each other. When he passed a mirror he looked at himself and saw that his face glowed like everyone else's. When he turned away from the mirror, Laura was gone. She had disappeared into some part of the party without him.

He found himself in a room bathed in red light at the edge of a throng of dancers. Someone handed him a glass of beer. He gulped it down and felt warm inside as the alcohol spread through his body. He felt at ease then, welcome, and familiar though he still didn't know where he was or why he was there. Each time his glass was empty he was handed a new one. The beer tasted like molasses. Gladly leaned back against a wall and moved to the beat of the music.

He scanned the room with his eyes and met the eyes of others. Some looked away when they saw him looking. Others looked at him, leaned over to the person next to them and said something that made that person look at him too. As the dancers moved past, some of them raised their arms or leaned against his body with theirs, trying to get him to join them. He preferred to stay where he was, though, leaning against the wall a while longer before moving on to explore the party further.

He was drinking from his sixth or seventh glass of beer when a woman with long, brown hair brushed past him, turned, looked into his eyes and said, "I remember you from the mountain." Gladly smiled and nodded, trying to act as if he remembered her, but he didn't and told her that he didn't know what she was talking about. She looked at him with disappointment in her eyes.

Laura walked out of the room into which the other woman had disappeared and took him by the hand. She led him to a door at the side of the house and into the forest. Laura held a torch above her head to light their way.

They arrived at what Laura said would be their only stop, a cabin in the middle of the forest that served as a bakery for the forest people. Gladly could not remember his last full meal and the smell of simple bread overwhelmed him. He fell to the ground. When he opened his eyes, it was dark again. He felt like he was going to die. Stars glittered through the tree branches above his head. He was at the edge of a field bordered on all sides by rows of tall old pine trees. The moon was full and white behind a veil of fog.

Gladly looked but saw no movement anywhere on the field. He walked out onto the untouched snow. Laura was nowhere in sight. He wondered where she had gone and why she had abandoned him after leading him so far into the forest. He wondered how far they had carried him from the bakery before laying him in the snow and thought to go back and look for footprints. When he returned to the spot, though, and looked down, he saw nothing in the snow but the imprint of his body.

Gladly turned and walked until he was in the middle of the field, where he stopped and stood to look around. The field stretched for a half mile in every direction. It appeared to be perfectly square, the pine trees around its edges like walls of a room that bent and swayed in the breeze. The stars and aurora-ringed moon were the room's ceiling.

Gladly heard a sound in the distance. Faint at first, it grew louder as it came nearer to the field. A flock of geese in a perfect V flew through the moon like an arrow striking the bull's eye of its target, disappeared behind the forest's wall of trees and continued on into the distance.

Gladly walked from the field and found a path that led through the woods to a clearing in which a small house had been built. The corn that had once grown next to the house was dead, its stalks brown and sprawled like bodies after a skirmish in random arrangement. Gladly walked along the edge of the field and found a wood trough filled with dark, oily water. Despite the cold, the water was not frozen.

Gladly looked down and saw a perfect reflection of the full moon that seemed to be clearer than the moon itself above. Gladly turned and followed his footsteps back to the spot in the snow where he had first found himself, lay down in the hollow his body had made, and closed his eyes. When he opened them again he was on the ground in front of the bakery. Laura stood above him.

"It's all right," she said, "You fainted." The strong arms of strangers reached down to help Gladly up. They carried him into the bakery and set him down on top of a pile of sacks that ran the entire length of one wall. Although they were filled with hard potatoes that bulged and pressed into his back, the sacks felt more comfortable than any mattress he had ever slept on. He tried to remember the last time he had a good night's sleep. He certainly hadn't slept a single sound night during his months in the trenches. The time before that seemed distant and too far away to think about.

Gladly wanted to return to the train station. He wanted to ride the train back to the town. He wanted to walk to the red horse and ride it back to the painting. He wanted to step through the painting and back to the schoolhouse and the world outside its door. He wanted to continue on his way.

The cabin was warm and filled with an orange glow, the smell of cinnamon, baking bread, and potatoes. A doorway led through the cabin's back wall to another room where the ovens were kept hot. Sacks of potatoes were piled against the wall to his left and right. People sat and dozed in chairs around a wood burning stove in the middle of the room. Others sat around two long tables and ate or rested their heads in their hands. A few, like Gladly, were sprawled on top of the potato sacks. One of them was asleep and snored loudly. The other smoked from a white clay pipe and stared at the ceiling with happy, thoughtful eyes.

Laura emerged from the kitchen with a tray of food, set it down on the table and motioned for Gladly to eat.

"Who are these people?" he asked.

"Most of these people are potato lifters," Laura said. "They've come a long way through the snow to bring the bakery its winter supply."

Gladly sat down and looked at his food. There was a mug of steaming hot cider, a small loaf of brown bread, butter, apricot jam, and a bowl of mashed potatoes. He dug into the potatoes with a wooden spoon and moaned with pleasure when the first taste touched his tongue. They were spiced with cinnamon, apple, and a hint of mustard. When he was finished with the potatoes, he tore the loaf of bread in half and spread butter and apricot jam on both sides. He closed his eyes as he chewed, and when he was finished with the bread, he raised the mug of hot cider to his lips and drank slowly.

When he was finished, Laura led him through the kitchens. The heat from the ovens made him yawn. His whole body was tired. All he wanted to do was sleep. He followed Laura with his eyes half closed. She took him from the bakery through the snow to a house a few hundred feet away. They walked through a door and entered a room. Gladly could barely keep his eyes open.

One second, he was standing next to a bed. The next, he was in the bed, beneath its clean blankets. Laura was next to him. Her body was warm against his, and for the first time since the start of the war, Gladly knew he would survive the night. He closed his eyes, let out a deep sigh, and fell asleep.

FOUR

The next morning, Laura poked his chest with her finger to wake him up. Gladly opened his eyes, yawned, and smiled. More snow had fallen during the night. Gladly and Laura ate heavy biscuits and the same potato dish Gladly had eaten the night before. When the plates and bowls were empty, Laura told Gladly to get dressed and meet him outside. She left the room and closed the door behind her. Gladly sat on the edge of the bed and stared at his feet, his hands, and the room around him. He tried to memorize everything. It was a simple room. A mirror in a cherry wood frame was all that hung on any of its white walls. Underneath the mirror was a table on which sat a pitcher of water, a glass, and a wash basin. Gladly poured some water into the basin, splashed it onto his face and rubbed the sleep from his eyes. He stood at the window for a minute and looked outside. The sky was dark and gray. A foot of snow had fallen in the night. The tree branches were heavy with snow and hung like tired arms at their sides. A slight breeze was blowing, enough to wiggle a branch and send its load tumbling to the ground. Gladly took a last look at the room and stepped outside, where Laura stood with a group of the potato lifters. She waved him over and pointed to what looked like a small boat covered with a shiny brown leather blanket.

"We're going sledding," Laura said. The potato lifters, six of them in all, stood like pallbearers about to lift a coffin at a funeral, bent down and picked the sled up off the ground. Laura and Gladly walked behind them down a path through the woods. Gladly looked back through the trees and caught one last glimpse of the house where they had spent the night. Laura held his hand and pulled him forward. They walked for what felt like an hour.

The path through the woods opened up to a clearing on the side of a hill with two rows of trees on either side that made it feel as if they were walking down the center aisle of a cathedral towards the altar. At the end of the clearing, the ground dropped off and fell into a steep, mile-long hill. The potato lifters stood and sat to the side of the sled and stared at the view.

Gladly and Laura joined them and looked too. All was quiet except for the steady breeze. At the bottom of the hill was a huge open field that stretched for several miles before the trees began again. Beyond the trees, in the distance, hills rose and rolled beneath their new blanket of snow. Dark gray billowy clouds sailed across the sky like elephants moving tail to tail on the horizon. Sunrays fell to the ground and made pools of light on the sides of the distant hills.

One of the potato lifters sneezed and startled all of them from their reverie. The ones who had been sitting stood and helped the ones who were standing with the sled. Gladly stood to the side with his arm around Laura's waist. They watched as the potato lifters untied the knots that had kept the leather covering drawn tight around the sled. When the final knot was released and the leather pulled back, Gladly saw that he had been wrong to think that the sled was a sled. When the last knot was untied and the covering removed, the thing underneath unfolded like a sheet of molasses and breathed.

The creature looked like the bottom of a boat with wings. It had two orange eyes that stared expressionless into the sky. Gladly turned to question Laura about the creature but she was gone. All but one of the potato lifters remained. The rest had disappeared into the forest. Gladly took a few steps in that direction, but the potato lifter held him back.

He led Gladly to the animal's side and stepped onto its back. He held an arm out, gesturing for Gladly to do the same. Gladly stepped lightly onto what felt like a thick rubber mat. The animal felt like one huge tensed muscle. The potato lifter pressed down on Gladly's shoulders to make him sit. He showed Gladly where to put his hands. There were ridged furrows like grooves in the animal's hide. Gladly gripped them as he would the rail on a tram, and when the potato lifter saw that Gladly was seated properly, he stepped off the creature's back, and watched as it and Gladly began their slide down the long hill.

The potato lifter pursed his lips and looked off to his left, in the direction of the distant hills. What Gladly could not know was that the man had raised the animal from birth, and that Laura, along with some of the other potato lifters, had persuaded him to let Gladly use it to get away.

Gladly did not know the animal's name, but like everything else that had happened to him since the war began, he did not think anything was strange anymore, just that some things had names and words that could be used to describe them while others had no names and no words.

After picking up speed, the animal lifted its head, raised its wings and sailed into the sky. He gripped the animal's furrows tight but was not afraid. Whenever he lost his grip for a moment or slid from one end of the animal's back to the other, it curled beneath him and bent itself so that he was always balanced perfectly in the middle where he could not fall off. The animal rose into the sky and glided with the wind. Gladly watched as the distant hills grew near. He wondered where they were going. He wanted to believe that the journey would take him someplace he could call its end and that there, wherever that end was, waited a place and a state of mind where he could take stock of all he had seen and all he had learned in the course of his travels. He pictured himself becoming a cartographer, spending his hours patiently making adjustments, redrawing borders, sketching the countries within the countries that existed but had never been marked on any map. He pictured an atlas or a book of maps that could be viewed in layers like the strata of the rocks in the earth. On top would be the physical world with its countries and border lines. He did not know how many other layers there would be, but he would start by charting out the states of mind he had experienced in different parts of the world. He knew that this layer of the map would be different for everyone but that it would also be a way to discover fellow travelers who had experienced similar states of mind during their journeys across similar parts of the map.

A gust of wind brought Gladly out of his daydream. They seemed to be entering a storm. Perhaps sensing that it was too dangerous to continue on in the face of the oncoming clouds, the winged thing banked into the wind and flew Gladly gently to the ground. Five feet above a snowy field, it stalled in mid-air, flexed its back, and dumped Gladly into a snow drift. Then, with a flap of its wings, it caught a breeze and rose up into the sky, banked, caught another updraft and flew on in the direction from which they had come. An hour later, the potato lifter would look up and see it descend from the sky. It would land tired from its trip to the distant hills and back. He would feed it several bowls of potato mash, wrap it in its canvas blanket, and lay it to rest near the fire in the bakery house to sleep.

FIVE

Gladly sat in the snow where he had been spilled and watched the creature fly off in the direction from which they had come. It banked into the wind and became a dot in the sky. He stood up, shook the snow from his clothes, and surveyed his surroundings. He was in the middle of yet another field but this time he was not entirely without bearings because he could see the tops of some houses sticking out from behind a stand of small trees to his left. He began to walk towards them, but stopped when he heard voices ahead of him.

He squatted down in the snow to make himself small and even though he knew there would be no way to escape the clear shot that would come if they saw him, he was prepared to bolt towards the trees. His stomach tightened when he saw four figures emerge from the trees at the edge of the field, but he relaxed a bit when he saw they were followed by four boys. They walked towards the middle of the field and stopped a hundred yards from where Gladly crouched in the snow.

Two of the men removed packs from their backs and began to arrange things they took from them in the snow. When they had taken out everything they needed, the four boys gathered around and set about assembling the pieces of some kind of contraption while the four men, who Gladly assumed were their fathers, stood to the side and watched.

Gladly could see their breath in the cold air, but he could not hear what they were saying. Ten minutes passed like this until finally the four boys stood up and stepped away from their work, giving Gladly a clear view of what they had been putting together. It was a rocket.

Gladly stood up, forgetting that he was trying to not be seen, and put his hands in his pockets to wait for the launch. The fathers and their sons turned towards him and appeared startled by his sudden appearance. He stared back at them without moving. He didn't know what he should do and was angry with himself for giving away his position.

One of the boys pointed at Gladly. Another one tugged at the leg of his father's pants and said something. His father brushed his hand away, whispered some kind of admonition, and took a step forward so that his son was behind him looking around his legs as if he were standing behind a tree. The four men and four boys stared at Gladly while Gladly stared back at them. Finally, Gladly decided that it would be best if he risked movement. He raised his hand slowly and waved. The four men nodded their heads in acknowledgement and waved back. Apparently satisfied that the man in the middle of the field was there only because he was curious about the rocket launch, they turned their attention back to their endeavor.

One of the boys ran a wire from the rocket to a firing device twenty feet away. After they made some final adjustments to the rocket, which stood in the snow like a finger pointing towards the sky, the boys and their fathers stood in a group to the side and watched as it shot into the sky. It made a hissing sound as it climbed and left behind a cloud of white smoke that enveloped the group of rocket launchers. The boys shouted with excitement and jumped up and down in the snow while their fathers clapped each other on the back and shook hands. Gladly smiled and watched as the rocket flew skyward.

It flew higher and higher until it was just a dot like the flying creature that had dropped Gladly in the middle of the field. A white parachute opened and the rocket floated slowly towards the ground. The wind took it away from its launch site and towards the woods. Gladly watched as the boys ran laughing underneath the rocket and its parachute. Three of the four men took out pipes and smoked as they walked slowly behind their sons.

Gladly stood with his hands in his pockets until the eight figures disappeared into the woods. His stomach growled. He turned and walked towards the houses on the hill, hoping they were part of a village where he could get something to eat. As he walked, Gladly thought about the things that had happened to him since he ran from the battlefield. He no longer felt afraid. He was simply curious to know what was going to happen next.

Gladly sighed and told himself to stop thinking about things that were out of his hands. When he reached the top of the hill, he saw that the houses had all been bombed. Their frames still stood but their insides were gutted and filled with rubble. Gladly pushed against the half-open door of one of the destroyed houses and stepped inside. Its four walls were still standing but the roof was gone, which made the sky look like the ceiling.

Three pigeons perched and cooed on the one remaining beam that leaned precariously against a wall. Gladly wondered who had lived there and what had happened to them. He crouched down in the rubble and ran his fingers across the fallen stones. He lifted a brick and found a silver locket. He opened it and looked inside. A picture of Elizabeth stared back at him. A strand of her hair was pressed behind the locket's glass. Gladly tried to memorize the expression on her face. She looked so melancholy that she appeared to be almost expressionless. He lifted another brick and found a silver pocket watch. He held it up to his ear and shook it.

The watch came to life for a few seconds but as soon as Gladly looked at it, the watch died again and fell into silence. He shook it but to no avail. He slipped it into one of his pockets along with the locket and stood up.

A woman's voice said, "It's yours. Keep it."

Gladly turned around slowly. He had been surprised too many times in the course of his journey to act startled now, so he was not surprised to see Elizabeth standing there framed by the door to the empty shell of the broken house. She wore the brown pants and work shirt that most of the potato lifters wore. Her hair fell across one side of her face in a chaotic tangle. She shook her head and flipped it away so Gladly could see both of her glowing sapphire eyes.

"This was my house," she said. Gladly stepped out of the rubble and through the door. "Everyone in my family was away when the bombs fell, except for my younger brother. The locket was his."

Gladly raised his hand to his chest and touched the locket through his shirt. His face flushed with sadness. He wanted to return the locket to her, but when he began to unbutton his pocket, Elizabeth reached forward and took his hand in hers. She led him away from the house and said, "I told you. The locket is yours. We will speak no more of it."

They walked in silence, hand in hand past the rows of destroyed and abandoned houses. The town, Elizabeth told him, had been overrun. Its inhabitants, those who were not killed during the initial assault, had fled and did not wish to return. Those who had survived packed up their belongings and left during the night. "Where?" he asked. Elizabeth nodded down the road that lay in front of them at their feet. It traveled into the distance for a while, disappeared behind a hill, and reappeared at the top of another.

"When?" he asked.

"A week ago," Elizabeth said. Gladly was about to ask if this was the day he had met her at the train station with Laura and Rachel, but she seemed to read his mind again and nodded before he could speak.

"You may have seen some of the refugees on the roads or on the train."

"A week," Gladly thought, and stared down the road. He had been gone for a week. If he could make it to the town where he first boarded the train, it was only a little further to home.

Elizabeth whistled. A black dog ran from behind a low stone wall in front of a house untouched by the advancing troops. Elizabeth let go of Gladly's hand and bent down to pet the dog.

"This is where I lived," she said.

"Where did they go from here?" Gladly asked. Again, Elizabeth pointed down the road and Gladly remembered seeing soldiers walking among the hordes of refugees trying to get out of town and away from the danger. Elizabeth led him inside. The dog followed. There was little in the way of furniture in the house, a table and two chairs in one room, a bed in the other. All of the walls were bare, stripped by looting soldiers. Nails where paintings once hung were all that remained. The black dog lay down at Gladly's feet and closed its eyes. Gladly noticed that it was no longer cold outside.

He looked out a window and saw that all of the snow was gone. Its disappearance had escaped him, another detail the had overlooked or did not know how to see. Just a half an hour earlier he had been dropped off in the middle of a snowy field and now, at the top of the hill where the remains of a town lay broken and vacant, the snow and cold air were gone and had been replaced with the first subtle hints of spring. So much seemed to have passed him by.

At the same time, other things had made themselves clear and still others, he knew, would only become clear later when he had time to think about them.

Elizabeth sat at the table and pointed towards the room with the bed. "You should rest for a while," she said. "but you can't stay here long, you must move on."

Gladly nodded in agreement. He did not want to stay, he wanted to keep moving, but he knew that it would do him some good to just sit still for a little while longer before setting out again. He walked into the room and closed the door behind him. He sat down on the edge of the bed and looked out the window. He listened to his breathing and the creaking of the bedsprings beneath him.

In the other room, Elizabeth picked up a guitar and strummed softly on its strings. Gladly folded his hands in his lap and sighed a deep sigh.

He wanted to sleep, rest, wake up and stay in the house with Elizabeth, but at the same time, he did not want to close his eyes, he just wanted to keep going. He was tired from his journey but with the road to the town in sight, he knew he was strong enough to make it the rest of the way. He did not know if he should feel safe with Elizabeth, but he did. His experience with Rachel had been terrifying. He was not sure how he felt about his time with Laura. She had shown him so many things that he still did not understand.

He imagined himself looking in the window from outside and pictured himself sitting on the bed, looking towards the window. He saw the bed, the bare walls, the closed door. He saw the door open and Elizabeth walk into the room. She leaned her guitar against the wall and sat down next to him on the bed. She put her arms around his shoulders and he let himself rest his head against hers. They sat like that for an hour. His eyes were filled with contentment. For the length of that hour, Gladly knew that he was immortal, that the moment would always be there, frozen in time.

Gladly had not thought about time that way before. Time was an ocean, he realized. He pulled the pocket watch from his pocket and held it to his ear. It was ticking, moving forward, and he was moving forward with it. Elizabeth kissed him on the cheek and smiled.

"You must go," she said.

He saw himself open Elizabeth's front door. He saw himself step outside and onto the road. He saw Elizabeth and the black dog framed in the doorway of their little house. He saw himself wave to them and turn towards the road. He heard horns blowing in the distance and he knew that he must follow their sound. They called to him and he walked down the road without looking back.

SIX

Gladly walked until he came to a bridge that had been blown up and no longer connected one side of the river with the other. He climbed down an embankment to the edge of the water and hopped from stone to stone until he was across and stood on the opposite bank. He looked at the bridge's stone foundation that remained intact and jutted out from the dirt on either side of the river and wondered if anyone would ever rebuild it. He climbed to the top of the bank and returned to the road. He passed by many empty houses and many fields absent of both their herds and their farmers.

Flies swirled around the rotting carcasses of dead cows, and when he came to a farmhouse just off the road, Gladly saw that along with a few dead pigs and chickens, the ground was littered with human bodies as well. It looked as if they had been lined up against the farmhouse wall and shot. Gladly wanted to stop and bury the dead, but something told him to keep walking.

He walked quickly until the dirt road narrowed into a path as it through the forest at the bottom of the hill he had seen in the distance from Elizabeth's house. Once he was in the woods, Gladly walked slowly and listened to the sounds of the forest. He listened to the birds as they chirped and hopped from branch to branch and rustled in the leaves on the ground while looking for food. The air was cooler in the woods than it had been on the road, as if winter had retreated into the forest like a battalion waiting to attack.

Gladly shivered and wondered how deep the forest was and how far he would have to walk before he found himself at the top of the second hill he had seen in the distance, the one behind which he hoped would be the town he first set out from by train. Gladly came to a huge rock standing in the middle of the path. It looked to him as if it had been rolled, pushed, or dragged from somewhere else. The ground to one side was scarred with boot prints and wagon tracks.

Gladly decided this was as good a place as any to stop and take a short rest. The rock stood six feet tall and ten feet wide. Gladly pulled himself up to its top and sat down. Pulling his knees up to his chest to rest his chin on his kneecaps, he rocked back and forth and hummed softly to himself with his eyes closed. He had enjoyed his stay with Elizabeth, but he was happy to be on the road and felt like he was heading in the right direction, even though it was only a hunch that the road would lead him where he needed to be.

When he opened his eyes, Gladly heard a noise from somewhere in the woods. Low at first, it grew in intensity until Gladly was sure that he was actually hearing something, and that what he was hearing were the horns that had called to him in his head when he set out a few hours earlier. He stood up on the rock and tried to determine which direction the sounds were coming from. It was not music he heard, but a droning that reminded him of a ship's horn blowing offshore in morning fog.

Gladly wanted to find the source of the horns, he wanted to know what they meant. Were they a signal to one of the armies or the people of the local villages and farms? Or were they a signal just for him? Gladly jumped down from the rock and set off running towards the sound of the horns. He ran in and out of trees, jumped over fallen branches, and tripped a few times on sticks that were hidden by dead leaves. He ran as fast as he could, and when he came to a small clearing, he thought he saw several men disappear into the trees on the other side. He ran across the clearing, and when he was halfway across, something hit him in the leg, causing him to fall to the ground. He rolled around in pain, his face red from the effort of trying not to scream. His pants were soaked with blood but he couldn't tell if he'd been shot or hit by some other kind of projectile.

He tried to crawl towards the cover of the forest, but as soon as he moved something came flying towards him through the air. For a moment he thought it was a bird, but as it came closer, Gladly saw that it was a grenade. He stood up and tried to dive out of its path. There was a flash of light and something hit his face before he slipped into shock. When he came out of it, he found himself sitting on a beach.

Gladly looked up and down the shore. His leg was bleeding and he was blind in one eye. To his left the beach stretched into the distance. To his right, a white tent stood swaying in the sea wind, its flaps waving its arms at him.

Gladly stood and limped to the tent's entrance. He stepped inside. On the left side of the tent a wooden table had been set. On the right side was an operating table, behind which stood a doctor in a white smock.

"Hello," he said, "Shall we eat first?" The doctor motioned for Gladly to sit. Gladly sat on a chair and took off his shoes. He dug his feet into the sand. It was soft and cool. The doctor sat across from him and offered Gladly bread. Gladly tore a chunk from the loaf and used it to soak up the thick bean soup in his bowl.

"I'm very tired," he said. The doctor looked at him for a few minutes without speaking. Waves crashed against the shore. Gladly looked up from his soup. The inside of the tent was bathed in white light.

"You've come a long way," the doctor finally said, eating his soup slowly, watching Gladly the whole time. "You deserve to be tired. But in the morning, you will be in a lot of pain. I don't want you to be afraid."

"Afraid of what?" Gladly asked. Something moved at Gladly's feet. He looked under the table. A child had crawled across the sand and leaned against one of the table's legs.

"My son," the doctor said, "two years old."

"Where is his mother?" Gladly asked. The doctor lowered his eyes.

"It's time we got started," he said. "Come with me." He led Gladly to the operating table on the other side of the tent. The doctor covered him with a white sheet and turned to put his operating smock and mask on. "There there," the doctor said. "Don't talk, just listen. I'll tell you a story." The doctor leaned into his work and spoke the familiar words of his story as Gladly drifted into a dream-like state.

"They said it would come to this, that our cities would be read about in the newspapers of distant countries, that we would die in each other's arms. We knew all along what we were getting into, and yet we did nothing to stop it from happening."

"My son-in-law died in my daughter's arms. Soon after that, the soldiers came to take her away. Where is she now? I don't know. Where did she disappear? Maybe she is alive in the hills, or like the birds that once came to our village's monastery during their migration, maybe she is further away than any of us is able to imagine. Perhaps she is alive, but simply too frightened to return. When my son-in-law died, we named a fountain after him, but for her we waited."

"Our monks strapped white flags to their backs, hoping for safe passage across the battlefields so they could bring the dead home who waited patiently in the sun while birds picked away at their bodies. My father carried a fistful of spent shell casings in his pocket and waited for the monks to return from their work every day. With each death, he removed a shell from his left pocket and slipped it into his right. Our village's women and children, the widows, mothers, and grandmothers, gathered each night next to Rainer's Fountain to hear the count. Our young boys looked at him with a strange curiosity in their eyes, waiting to take the places of their brothers who had fallen.

"One day, a scout who had been sent out with my daughter's picture in hand returned to the village with some information about what had happened to her. They took her into the hills and raped her near the place where the stream emerges from the trees at the bottom of the hills to begin its descent into town. A boy from our village saw it all happen from the rocks above and led our scout back to the place where the soldiers had left her for dead. When he got there, though, she was gone."

"Among the many boot prints in the dust, there were two smaller footprints that led towards the hills. She did not return to the village. I imagine my daughter lying in the dust. An hour in and out of consciousness. Gunshots in the distance, execution volleys. She moves and opens her eyes, rises and walks to the trees. She pulls a leaf from a branch and puts it in her mouth to get rid of the taste of blood. Her arms are caked with dust. She goes to the stream, takes off her torn dress, and moans in pain as the water washes over her body. Her sweat and blood join the current, are pulled downstream, towards the village, towards Rainer's Fountain at the center of the square. She hears a young boy's voice from behind the rocks near the stream."

"Soldiers coming," he says.

"She blinks and rubs water from her eyes, rises from the stream, grabs her dress from the rock and runs with it in hand to the boy's side. He leads her to a narrow passage in the rock face. The path weaves in and out of stone and finally ends at the mouth of a cave. Inside, the boy lights a candle. They hear shots somewhere outside. The cave is littered with bones. A skull smiles at them."

"Get dressed," the boy says. He takes a cigarette from a small metal box he has stashed among the bones and lights it as she slips into her dress."

"She sits next to him on the ground and thinks for a moment about Rainer, the way he smoked cigarettes on their balcony before the war, the way the moonlight fell on the branches of the olive trees in front of their house, and how Rainer's face appeared in the orange glow of his cigarette every time he inhaled."

"I'll draw a map for you," the boy says, and digs his finger into the sand at their feet. "Look," he says, "here is the cave. Here, the stream, here the minefield. Snipers, path, cemetery, town. You must go back. You must go now."

"She looks back at him for a moment from the mouth of the cave, turns and begins to run. The valley appeared to her as it did on the floor of the cave, but she has forgotten where the boy told her to go. She continues to run anyway, thinking that what she is supposed to do, where she is supposed to go, who she is to meet will be clear eventually."

"As she ran she thought about a series of dreams she had when she was a young girl. She used to dream about a boy who lived far away, across an ocean. Sometimes she crossed the sea to wake him. Other times he came to wake her. At first, they just stared at each other until one of them yawned and returned to their own bed, but one night, the boy sneezed and she laughed. The boy asked her why she was laughing."

"Because you sneezed," my daughter said, "and because I never imagined you would sneeze in one of my dreams."

"So you are also dreaming of me?" he asked.

"Yes," she said, and you are dreaming of me. They looked at each other for a while longer until she began to feel tired and yawned. Without saying anything to each other, they closed their eyes and drifted back to sleep."

"Sometimes when she woke up in the morning to go to school, she felt as if the boy was next to her in bed, but when she woke completely the feeling disappeared and she got up to get ready for school."

"One night when they found each other in a dream she told him that she had begun to think of him when she was awake and that she looked for him wherever she went."

"I look for you too," the boy admitted. "Sometimes I see someone from a distance who looks like you. I run after her, but it is never you." The boy leaned forward to hold her in his arms but, as happened each time they began to feel close, they drifted back to sleep and were pulled apart."

"One night, she told him that she thought it would be the last night they met in their dreams. They stared at each other in silence, trying to memorize each other's face. The boy suggested they come up with a sign to greet each other if they ever met someone in the waking world who resembled them."

"And even if it isn't me," she told him when they had agreed on the sign, "signal anyway, to be sure."

"I will," the boy said, and leaned forward to kiss her. When their lips touched they were pulled apart, and never dreamed each other again."

"As she runs through the valley, she thinks about Rainer and how he had laughed when she told him about the dream, how he feigned jealousy whenever she pointed out someone on the street who resembled the boy. As she runs, she tells herself to stop thinking about the past and count her footfalls. Not knowing how long she must run, she knows that the number of steps needed to get there is finite and that to know that she has arrived where she is supposed to be, she must not lose count."

"She arrives at the cemetery and sees a line of the dead walking down the hill towards the shore, towards the water. They are dressed in white, each with a small bird was perched on their shoulder, and each with an object in their hands, a music box, a kaleidoscope, a watch on a silver chain, a necklace, a bracelet, a ring, a locket, a box inside a box... They disappear into the sea and my daughter turns away."

"A line of monks advances into the square to pray with the women and light candles. One of them pauses in front of my father. He hands him an ancient pistol and a box of shells. My father drops his cane and takes the pistol in one hand, the box of shells in the other. He loads the pistol and waits for a signal. Shots echo from the hills."

"Our women walk towards the advancing soldiers in a line with candles lit, daring them to shoot. The monks, with their white flags, are not far behind, but they are concealing rifles beneath their robes. Our women, when they see that the soldiers are not going to shoot, jump on them with knives. The monks raise their rifles and shoot."

"My son-in-law Rainer advances towards the hill. He is surrounded by a small army of boys who laugh and throw stones at the frightened soldiers. My father walks forward, waves to Rainer and laughs. Rainer points towards the open plain of the desert. In the fading light of dusk, they can just make her out, a lone figure in a torn dress. She is running with long strides, pulling in the night behind her as she gets closer to the hill. It's my daughter. She is followed by a cloud of white chalk, a line of charging elephants, and robed holy men covered in dust. The dream ends. I wake up. My daughter is nowhere."

The doctor fell silent and wrapped bandages around Gladly's leg. He placed a patch over Gladly's blind eye and wrapped more bandages around his head to keep the patch in place.

"I'm finished, " the doctor said.

Gladly slid off the operating table and limped towards the entrance of the tent. The sun was still bright, but he was no longer on the shore, no longer near the sea. He was in the middle of a field. The red horse stood nearby, watching him. An empty picture frame floated in mid-air a few feet above the ground. The horse whinnied and Gladly limped forward. The frame shimmered and began to fade.

He heard a train whistle in the distance. A nurse injected something into his arm that made him feel warm and like he was floating through air. He closed his eyes.

A bee buzzed outside the window and tapped against the glass. Gladly knew that he was at least halfway home.